audition speeches
for women

EDITED BY JEAN MARLOW   **SECOND EDITION**

A & C Black • London

To Brian Schwartz thank you

Second edition 2005
Reprinted 2007
A&C Black Publishers Limited
38 Soho Square
London W1D 3HB
www.acblack.com

ISBN 978-0-7136-7413-2

© 2005, 2001 Jean Marlow

First edition published 2001

A CIP catalogue record for this book is available from the
British Library

This book is produced using paper made from wood
grown in managed, sustainable forests. It is natural,
renewable and recyclable. The logging and manufacturing
processes conform to the environmental regulations of
the country of origin.

Typeset in 10 on 12 pt Garamond and 9 on 11 pt DIN

Printed and bound in Great Britain by
Creative Print and Design (Wales), Ebbw Vale

Jean brought to my attention while she was preparing this new edition of *Audition Speeches for Women* that musicals seemed to represent one of the biggest sources of work for actors, if the current productions in London are any indication (twenty one musicals, fifteen plays). Perhaps this should give a heightened significance to Jean Hornbuckle's and Barry Grantham's advice (see pages 6 and 7). Of course you can sing, maybe you just need to work at it a little more! 'Explore your potential'.

However we are still spoilt for choice with a variety of current productions in and around London, such as *Blithe Spirit, Journey's End, The Woman in Black*, the Hampstead Theatre's production of *Losing Louis*, the Royal Shakespeare Company's *King Lear*, the continuous high standard of productions at our local 'gem' the Tricycle Theatre and dare I say it, the ever so 'avant-garde' production of *Sex Addict* at the Royal Court Theatre Upstairs!

As I write the Royal National Theatre is presenting a revival of Lorca's *The House of Bernarda Alba* and I am reminded of Lorca's own definition of theatre as '*as school of laughter and lamentations ... The theatre is an extremely useful instrument for the edification of a country, and the barometer that measures its greatness or decline. A sensitive theatre, well orientated in all its branches, from tragedy to vaudeville, can alter a people's sensitivity in just a few years, while a decadent theatre where hooves have taken the place of wings can cheapen and lull to sleep an entire nation.*'

In this new edition Jean manages to introduce us to some of the 'laughter and lamentations'. Keep the wind beneath your wings and try to avoid the hooves!

With Jean I wish you all that's good – and great auditions!

EAMONN JONES
THE ACTORS' THEATRE SCHOOL

contents

audition speeches

acknowledgements

I would like to say thank you to the actors, directors, playwrights, casting directors, agents and publishers who have kindly contributed to this book.

In particular I would mention Athos Antoniades, Corinne Beaver, Tay Brandon, Frances Cuka, Kevin Daly, April De Angelis, Ellen Dryden, Gillian Diamond, Alison Gorton, John Higgins, James Hogan, Tesni Hollands, Rona Laurie, Lucia Latimer, Jacky Matthews, Katie Mitchell, Hannah Newman, John Quinlan (IT support), Keith Salberg, Carol Schroder, Don Taylor, Drew Rhys Williams. Also Brian Schwartz and Offstage Bookshop, and my editors, Jenny Ridout and Katie Taylor. And not forgetting my co-director, Eamonn Jones of The Actors' Theatre School, and the students themselves who tried out all these speeches for me.

preface

There are more new plays, more musicals, more adaptations and revivals – and more and more being demanded of actors all the time. We came into the new millenium with Alan Ayckbourn's *House & Garden* at the Royal National Theatre – two plays performed simultaneously within the same building, with actors running between the Olivier and Lyttleton stages to pick up their cues on time! Now, four years later at the National, we have *His Dark Materials* – based on Phillip Pullman's epic novels and adapted by Nicholas Wright into two full-length plays covering two nights and using the same cast. A new adaptation of *Whose Life Is It Anyway?* directed by Peter Hall, has opened at the Comedy Theatre with Kim Cattrall in the part originally played by Tom Conti – a demanding role for any actor!

Many of the extracts used in this new edition are from recent productions, some of them still running in London at the time of writing. Marina Carr's beautifully written *By The Bog of Cats* is still playing at Wyndhams Theatre and a revival of Noel Coward's *Blithe Spirit* has just opened at the Savoy Theatre, London.

All the speeches have been tried and tested by students from The Actors' Theatre School, either in workshops, at auditions, or in the London Academy of Music and Dramatic Art (LAMDA) or the New Era Academy examinations.

I have also invited teachers, examiners, a casting director, an agent and two professional actors to give advice on surviving in a competitive and sadly, overcrowded profession.

I hope these books will fulfil a need for both student and professional actors alike, and also be a reminder of the many good plays seen in London and the provinces – and often too briefly on the 'fringe'.

more about auditioning

You've made up your mind to become an actor. But before you can even begin you're faced with 'competition'. You apply for drama school, but first you have to be selected from what seems like hundreds of other people who all have the same idea. You have to **audition**. 'Fear of failure' starts to creep up on you. And you have to push it away, otherwise it can 'dog' you all the way through your life as an actor. An audition or 'casting' is not an examination or some sort of test to see who gets the highest grades. It may not seem fair at the time, but very often you just weren't what the auditioner, director or casting director was looking for. You didn't fit the bill.

A friend of mine, not long out of drama school, was touring in a production of *Spring and Port Wine* playing 'Hilda', the daughter of a strict father who is determined to make her eat a herring for dinner which she hates. Throughout the play the herring is put before Hilda at every meal, but she steadfastly refuses to eat it. Then the herring disappears and the family cat is suspected. The cat was played by a large ginger tom called Hughie – that only his owner could love. The show went well, the notices were good, and when a casting director came in on the second week of the tour, the actors had high hopes of getting 'something on television'. To everyone's astonishment the only actor offered a part was Hughie. The casting director was casting a cat food commercial. Suddenly Hughie had become a star and the film company sent a limousine to take him to the studios each day.

Always remember you haven't failed. You simply weren't selected – and in this case the cat got the job!

A musical director, who has sat through hundreds of auditions for West End musicals confirmed this. If someone arrives to audition and they are not what the director has in mind, they will probably be stopped after a few bars of music and sent away with a 'Thank you, we'll let you know.' The next artist to arrive may not be nearly as good, but will often get a recall because he or she looks right for the part.

A director is just as anxious to cast the right person as you are to get the job, particularly if he is putting on a whole season of plays. Does this actor look young enough to play down to seventeen, can this actress age from twenty to forty-five. Are they going to contrast well with the rest of the company who have already been cast? Should we be looking for a 'name'? It is not always the best actor or actress that gets the part. How can it be?

So throw 'failure' and 'rejection' out of your vocabulary. As long as you've done your very best to prepare for your audition, you haven't failed, you've simply added to your experience and may even be called back another time. Only the other day an actor telephoned to say he had just auditioned for a lead in the tour of *Joseph and the Amazing Technicolor Dreamcoat*. The director told him he was wrong for the part, but liked his audition and arranged to see him again for a new show being cast at the end of the month.

But let's have a look at the first audition you are most likely to encounter when you are thinking about 'going into the business' – the drama school audition.

the drama school audition

TIM REYNOLDS, Principal of the Academy Drama School, White-chapel, has this advice for would be drama students:

'I pondered for some time, wondering what could possibly be added to the advice already given in Jean's earlier books, *Actors'/Actresses' Audition Speeches – for All Ages and Accents*. Then I decided simply to put in writing the advice and help we give to those students who are on our one year Medallion Course – for seventeen to twenty year olds – which is solely dedicated to preparing them to audition for drama school, and for the reality of the three-year course they are hoping to enter.

First. Be very sure of your dedication. Drama schools are not about getting into television soap operas, or block-busting movies. They are more concerned with training your talents to the extent that you can rise to any challenge that may come your way. Although some actors achieve fame and fortune, most do not, and unless you feel sure that working regularly in the profession you love is sufficient reward, think again before you embark on a training you will probably never complete.

Do not undertake to audition for drama school until you feel entirely prepared. Although it is true to say that the people who are audition-ing you want to offer you a place, there is enormous competition from other applicants. If you come to your audition with a clear understand-ing of your speeches and a strong idea of what you want to do with them, that's half the battle. The Academy audition literally hundreds of prospective students each year, so we have a very good idea of what we are looking for. Here are a few tips which may be of help.

Audition for all the drama schools, even the ones that are not on the top of your list. The more auditions you attend the better you get at auditioning and the better your chances. If you decide that there is only one school you could possibly go to, and then don't get in you'll have to wait 'till next year to apply again, and this could go on until you collect your pension. Strike while the iron is hot, and increase your chances. You may get more than one offer, so you could have a choice. If you do, it's important that you go to the one in which you felt most comfortable at your audition.

Find out as much as you can about the school for which you are auditioning. Each school has its own criteria, and to an extent, its own method of training, and it is as well to know as much about that particular school as possible. For example, the Academy is most widely known for being the first full time evening and weekend drama school, training over six terms which are on average twelve weeks in length. This kind of information is available in the various prospectuses, which you should study with great care before your audition.

Look very carefully at the requirements for the audition, and make sure you follow them to the letter. There may well be a workshop. Listen carefully to the instructions given, and if there is anything you do not understand, you must ask. Always be in good time for your audition. Punctuality is essential in the acting business, and this must start with your training. Know your speeches thoroughly. Not just well enough to recall the lines, but so well that you can concentrate entirely on the character you are playing. You are likely to be asked to do the speech in an entirely different way, and time and again I have seen prospective students totally unable to recall the speech under such conditions.

The speeches from this book are chosen with care, but they are only a section of the play. What has your character done or lived through before the speech begins? What will he or she go on to do afterwards. It is vital that you read the whole play, not just because you will be asked questions on it, though you well might, but you yourself will have become familiar with the person you are playing. Every character must start with you, so it is important that you pick someone that you understand, who in other circumstances could be you. Do not choose a character too old, or too young, or whose experience of life is vastly different from yours. The auditioners only need a few lines to know whether you are right for them.

Should you get help with your speeches? Well, yes, I think you should, although some drama schools advise against it. They have seen all too many times the young hopeful before them spouting lines and carefully rehearsed gestures that have been drilled into them by someone whom the procession has passed by, and who would like to live again through you. The right tuition is important. The auditioners want to see your performance and a good tutor will help you realise your performance, rather than give you theirs.

There are one or two drama schools who supply a list of speeches from which to choose. It is not a good idea to do these speeches for other auditions because they are known to the other schools and it might appear that you are simply too lazy to learn another speech.

Finally, it is important to realize that the odds against you getting into any particular drama school of necessity are high, as they are when you have completed your training. The advice you are being given at the beginning of this book should be used to shorten those odds. At the end of the day, though, when you are turned down, remember it is only the decision of that particular school, and only at that particular time. Never lose confidence in yourself or your abilities.

The best of luck. If you've got the will, the heart and the stamina, combined of course with the talent, you'll get there.'

Robert Palmer, was at one time Senior Voice Tutor at the Royal Academy of Dramatic Art (RADA) which auditions between 1400 and 1500 students a year for 30 available places. He had this to say about the importance of a clear, audible voice:

'After auditioning for a place at the Royal Academy of Dramatic Art, workshops are held to determine further the technical and interpretive ability of selected candidates, particularly in a class situation.

On this occasion the Voice Department teachers give an individual ear-test where the candidate is required to sing/hum different notes played for them on the piano, sing a song and give a 'cold' reading of a text, also to participate in voice and speech exercises with a class.

During this the teacher is noting details of the actor's voice-quality, vocal range and speech, in particular any specific voice problems.

As these auditions draw in people from all over the world, the expectation has to be, as in any audition, that the actor is clearly audible and distinct – whatever their own particular dialect or accent.

Therefore it is essential that prior to the event the importance of maintaining a good standard of spoken delivery is realised. It is suggested that the regular practice of voice and speech exercises involving breath-support, resonance and articulation are necessary to underpin both classical and modern material used in the audition.'

working today in professional theatre

SIR PETER HALL created the Royal Shakespeare Company (which he ran from 1960–68) and directed the National Theatre from 1973–88. During that time he opened its new premises on the South Bank. After his repertory season at the Old Vic, he ran the Peter Hall Company in the West End until 1999 and has since opened his highly praised production of John Barton's *Tantalus* at the Denver Center for the Performing Arts in Denver, Colorado – transferring it to the Barbican Theatre, London in 2001. He has just directed *Whose Life Is It Anyway?* at the Comedy Theatre, London and has this to say about creative work in the theatre:

'Creative work in a theatre has always been done by a company. Here is another paradox. A company does the best work – but good work can also create a company. It may form itself by chance because a collection of actors in a commercial production have worked together in the past. Or it may be stimulated by the playwright's demands or the director's inspiration. It can happen in a matter of days. But the potent theatre company takes longer to develop, as actors grow together, learning each other's working habits, learning indeed how they dislike as much as how they like each other. Making theatre needs everyone to accept that they are dependent on everyone else. The messenger with one line can ruin the leading actor's scene if he does not speak at the right tempo and in the right mood. The wig-mistress who is late for a quick change can wreck the concentration of everyone on stage. Company work recognises dependency. Indeed it celebrates it . . . At the Old Vic with our small company of actors we found that the audiences' traditional responses were still strong: they loved seeing the same actors in different parts; they had an enthusiasm for seeing young talent develop; a feeling that the group had a strong and intimate relationship with it which was growing with every production. The more cohesive the company became, the more it felt capable of an immediate dialogue with its audience, and the more it felt able to arouse an imaginative response. This is the true process of live theatre.'

developing extra skills

More and more demands are being made upon actors today. In the *Equity Job Information News* actors and actresses were wanted for the excellent London Bubble Theatre's production of *Sleeping Beauty*. They had to be able to sing, play a musical instrument and jive. Without these extra skills, however good a performer you might be, there is no sense in even applying for an audition like this.

JACQUELINE LEGGO, agent and personal manager, submits artistes for theatre, film, television and radio and has clients working at the time of writing in the West End musical *Sweeney Todd*, the pantomime *Dick Whittington* in Liverpool, the television series *After Life* (ITV) and the feature films *Pride and Prejudice* and *Oliver*. She has this to say:

'When arranging interviews it is important to know that the performer is well equipped with contrasting audition speeches. It would be wonderful if we were always given enough time to prepare pieces which could be angled towards a particular job, but quite often an interview will be for the next day. If an artiste has a repertoire of speeches then the likelihood is that one of the pieces will be suitable. It is important to realise there is a great deal of competition for the available jobs and these days, with many musicals providing work, having one or two songs prepared as well, can only help open up opportunities. Any additional skills are certainly worth mentioning on your CV. For example playing a musical instrument, languages, fencing, horse riding – football has been asked for most recently for *Dream Team* – and driving a car is always a useful asset.'

JEAN HORNBUCKLE trained with the Royal Academy of Music. She is an opera and recital singer and coaches singers and actors for musicals:

'Actors are often requested to prepare a song – sometimes a particular style is specified, or it can be a free choice. Many find this daunting and doubt their singing is good enough, although with the help of a teacher, it is probable that they could acquit themselves perfectly adequately.

Musical ability of any sort is a definite advantage as it can open up opportunities for actors in more varied fields, particularly in musicals where small parts involve only a little singing.

Recently, a well known writer on musical affairs wrote an article bemoaning the dreadful standard of singing in West End shows at the moment, and asking where the good singers in this country are. It cannot be denied there is a real need for well trained singers to meet composers' requirements.

A good understanding of the singing voice and a secure technique are absolutely essential for sustaining a career in any type of music from pop and jazz through to serious classical, and only with proper training can the vocal stamina required to sustain a long run in a show be built up.

Prolonged misuse of the singing voice through ignorance of these things can lead to serious vocal problems affecting both singing and speaking voice, and it is worth considering having singing lessons both to learn about correct use of the voice, and also gain confidence to present a song successfully at an audition.'

BARRY GRANTHAM, author of *Playing Commedia*, performer, director and teacher specialising in Commedia dell'Arte and other forms of physical theatre, is also well aware of the additional skills expected of actors today:

'There was a time when all you needed was a small selection of modern and classical audition pieces, a good voice (with a 'Queen's English' accent of course), a few funny dialects, and, perhaps even more important than any of these, a good wardrobe; later you might need some talent but at least you knew where to start. Now you don't know where you are – there is a chance for a part in a prestigious production of *Timon of Athens*, but your agent tells you that you must be able to play the saxophone and drive a motorbike through a burning hoop. You know the '*Mercy*' speech from *Merchant of Venice* but can you act it while juggling five balls?

You cannot be ready for every quirky possibility but you can prepare for some of the things most likely to be demanded of you by today's theatre, where the straight play is a rarity rather than the norm (much of the repertoire of our National Theatre is devoted to musicals and other 'Total Theatre' productions).

First, perhaps, there is a much greater need to equip yourself by training in movement of all kinds: dancing, mime, stage fighting, acrobatics, period dance and styles, movement which indicates status, comedy and eccentric behaviour. It is a good idea too to treat seriously any time spent on preparation for a musical you may be involved in. You may never be or wish to be in a musical but the experience of its multiple demands will be invaluable. Masks are now often called for and there is a very specialized technique required for working in the different types of mask from the epic full masks of Greek theatre to the half-masks of Commedia dell'Arte. Then there is the whole area of improvisation, which in present training tends to concentrate on soul searching, character analysis on the Stanislavsky model – valuable but not of much help in the 'instant impro' so frequently part of today's audition process.

Perhaps surprisingly, if we look for an all embracing technique to provide us with a training that will fit us for these most recent requirements we cannot do better than to call upon that most ancient of disciplines, the Commedia dell'Arte – or more exactly *Commedia* – the shortened version now used to denote all the skills, but not necessarily involving the historic characters of Arlecchino, Colombina, Pantalone and so on. Here we have physical theatre at its most intense. Here is mask work, mime, movement, comedy, timing, audience communication, and instantaneous improvisation. It can incorporate any performing skill: dance, acrobatics, vocal and instrumental music, circus skills, all fitted into a dramatic framework that can be as truthful as anything demanded by the most dedicated followers of the Method (though its affinities are perhaps closer to Brecht and Grotowski). Unfortunately most drama schools give only a peripheral glimpse of Commedia at best, but gradually it is becoming evident that it should form a central element of any actor's training, sharing equal time with that devoted to Shakespeare, the modern masters, and the training approaches of both the Method style and traditional tuition.'

PENNY DYER, voice and dialect coach, trained on the teaching course at the Central School of Speech and Drama in the late seventies. Her most recent credits include *North and South* and *Blackpool* for BBC Television, the films *Dirty Pretty Things* and the Bafta-winning *The Deal*, both directed by Stephen Frears and the West End musicals *The Woman in White* and *My Fair Lady* both directed by Trevor Nunn. Penny works frequently for the Almeida, Donmar and Hampstead Theatres. She has just completed filming on *Mrs Henderson Presents*, with Judi Dench and Bob Hoskins directed again by Stephen Frears:

'Never use an accent for the accent's sake. It doesn't impress. Only use what is relevant to the character and the rhythms of the writing. Make sure you feel comfortable with the accent, so that it sits in your mouth with the same familiarity as when you wear a favourite coat. This is one very good reason to see a dialect coach. There are quite a few of us now and it pays to have that hour's worth of confidence building. Also, if you have been briefed to speak in a specific accent, but are unsure what that means, ask a dialect expert, we understand the 'lingo'. If you are asked to read a script in an accent, on the spot – so to speak – ask for five minutes preparation time and go elsewhere to do this, so that you can practice aloud, not in your head. Don't use a drama school audition as an 'Accent Show'. They want to hear the potential of your own voice and speech, so only choose to use an accent if you're really 'at home' with it. Try to master a few accents for your repertoire, especially a modern Received Pronunciation (RP). It acts as a physical springboard for all the rest.'

advice from the actors

I asked two actors, who have both left drama school within the past five years to give some tips on auditioning and tell us a bit about their own experiences:

SAMANTHA POWER trained at the Welsh College of Music and Drama and played 'Cecily' in the Number One Tour of *The Importance of Being Earnest*. On television she has appeared in *City Central*, *Cops* and *Peak Practice* and was 'Sonia' in the BBC Television sitcom *A Prince Among Men*. She also plays 'Lisa' in the film *Low Down* directed by Jamie Thraves.

'Auditions can be quite an intimidating experience, especially in the early stages of your career, but I believe they can often be quite exciting and enjoyable.

When you go up for a television audition you will usually meet the director, casting director and sometimes the producer. You are often required to read from the script so if sight-reading isn't your strong point – Practise!

It is important to find as much information about the role as possible – what the character is like, the general synopsis and style of the piece – all of which will create a clear picture in your mind and help prepare you for the audition. If you haven't had the luxury of being sent a script, make sure you arrive early enough to look through it.

I remember auditioning for a new BBC sitcom just six months out of drama school. I was sent the script in advance and I read it over and over again searching for clues as to what this character was like. I worked on it with the same approach I would any other role. I had the audition and was then recalled to meet the writers and the producer, and to read opposite the well-known lead actor. I was successful. Much later, I was told by one of the writers the reason I got the part was because 'You came into the room and made the character your own!' If you are prepared to work hard you will see the rewards.

If you are required to do a dialect, it is imperative you do it correctly. Any one of the people auditioning you could be from that area, so if you haven't prepared it could turn into a very embarrassing situation!

Always remember, if it doesn't work out the first time, don't be disillusioned. Decisions are based upon several factors. It is not necessarily a reflection on your ability to act!

So think positive. Be patient and Good Luck!'

MATT PLANT trained at the Academy Drama School. He recently played 'Algernon' in the Number One Tour of *The Importance of Being Earnest* and 'The Tutor' in *Anger* for BBC Television, directed by David Berry:

'Sometimes one is asked to travel long distances to an audition. This should never deter an actor as it could be 'the crock of gold at the end of the rainbow' and if it's not, you can always turn it down. Either way it can only add to your experience. At least that's what I thought as I walked into the Gaiety Theatre, Ayr in Scotland! I had already travelled all the way up from London by bus, thanks to the unfailing dedication of our beloved rail, had endured the dictates of Mrs Mince's 'Oh yes, all the stars stay here' boarding house, and was prepared for anything.

The audition panel, for it was a panel, wore suits and for a moment I thought perhaps I was being interviewed for Microsoft! 'Sing Happy Birthday', they said. 'What for?' I exclaimed, this being an audition for Terence Rattigan's *Murder in Mind*. I should have known when they asked if I could 'act like a mole' and 'talk like a farmer', and at this point produced a horse's head (papier mâché). It was only later I realised they had been considering me for 'future projects', whatever those projects were, and in actual fact the Rattigan play had already been cast!

The experience did not put me off auditions, or travelling long distances to get to them, although it has given me a strange aversion to horses! Funny that . . .'

auditioning for films and television

Even the most experienced actors will often tell you they have no idea why they got a particular film or television part or, why they didn't. What are film and television directors looking for? I was once told at a screen test, as I fumbled with the script I had just been handed by the casting director and tried to read it, at her request, without my glasses, 'Don't worry – it's really a 'look' they're looking for'!

So I passed this problem over to film and television casting direc-tor, DOREEN JONES, who cast the film *Orphans* for Peter Mullins, the television mini-series *Prime Suspect* and *Fingersmith*, a Sally Head Production for director Aisling Walsh:

'First thing to remember is that generally speaking (I can only speak for myself) you wouldn't be at the interview unless the casting director thought you were good. Nowadays with a very short run-up to the start of most film and television, there just isn't time to see the world and their mother. Generally I only suggest a few actors for each part but they will have been whittled down from an enormous list. I usually bring in three or four actors who represent different ways of playing the part.

If possible, try and find out a bit about the project. I would urge every actor to download the demo software from the internet (www.finaldraft.com). This enables them to read and print any scripts they may be being considered for. If the script is an adaptation of a book, direc-tors are impressed if you've taken the trouble to read the book – it shows commitment. Engage with the people you're meeting – it's no good leaning back in your seat trying to look cool – it looks as if you aren't interested; lean forward and show enthusiasm for the project – but don't go over the top. You may be asked to read – some actors have a facility for this and some don't. In order to give yourself the maximum chance, either arrive earlier so that you can familiarise yourself with the part or call the casting director the day before and ask if you can come in and pick up the lines or have them faxed to you. Only the churlish will refuse. This means that when you do read, you will be able to make eye contact with whoever is reading with you (usually the poor casting director) and again directors will be impressed that you have taken the trouble. Very often the director will say after just reading once, that was just fine. If you're not happy, ask to have one more go and ask if the director would like it a bit differently. Sometimes I would like an actor to have another go, but it's tricky for a casting director to intervene at this point – it could look as if they are undermining the director.

Occasionally you will be sent a script before a meeting. This is because the director finds it helpful to find out what your 'take' is on the script. So read it properly, not just once but several times so that you can talk intelligently and in depth about the character you have come in for. Make a note of not only the writer's notes and what your character says but also what other characters say about you. Do not, on any account arrive saying you didn't have time to read it properly. If that's the case, you might as well leave then because it's unlikely you'll get the part. If something catastrophic has happened in your personal life, and you genuinely have not been able to read the script, get on to your agent and see if you can be seen later. If you have had the script you should definitely learn the lines, not necessarily to the extent that you can put the script away but enough so that you don't have to constantly refer to it.

There are still some directors around who don't read actors. It may be that they prefer to rely on their 'gut' instinct or that they and the casting director have worked together many times and know each other's taste. In these cases it sometimes helps to talk about parts that you have played (subtly of course!) that may bear some resemblance to the character you have come in for. If you have come in for a character with an accent that is not your normal accent it is a good idea to think of a story to tell which involves you using the accent of that character.

There are lots of 'Chiefs' around these days and sometimes it is necessary when we 'Indians' have made a decision about who we would like to play the part, that we have to refer it upwards. This is when you will be asked back to go on video. So please think about the part you are videoing for. Don't have a late night if you're going to look wrecked the next day and that's not what the part calls for. It will be the first time the executives have seen you and no amount of us saying that you really are only twenty-three even if you're looking forty will convince them that we have made the right decision. You will not only have let yourself down, you will have let down those who had confidence in you as well.

When you don't get the part, try not to take it too personally. Remember that you wouldn't have been in for the interview if the casting director didn't think you were a good actor. More than likely, the decision will have been made on physical grounds i.e. family resemblance or a physical variation within a group so that the audience can distinguish one character from another.'

auditioning for voiceovers and radio drama

PATRICIA LEVENTON, Royal Shakespeare Company actress and former member of the BBC Radio Drama Company:

'Your voice can be your fortune. A good flexible voice coupled with the ability to sight-read is one of the greatest assets an actor can have. The world of commercial voiceovers both on radio and TV can be extremely lucrative. You have to be able to go into a studio, pick up a script, read it, time it and give the exact emphasis required by the advertiser. Often there are a great many words needing all your articulatory skills to fit them into the ten, twenty or thirty seconds of the average commercial.

Radio Drama is another great source of work. Most of the drama schools now enter their students for the Carlton Hobbs Award (named after the great radio actor of the 1940s, '50s and '60s). This competition takes place towards the end of the academic year, i.e. June, and six students are awarded a place with the BBC Radio Drama Company. They provide a talent base and are usually given a six-month contract enabling them to gain experience of the medium and supplying them with the opportunity to work alongside very experienced actors in the field. For these auditions it is advisable for students to work on their pieces in detail with their tutor as much in advance as possible. Choose pieces you feel at home with. The usual contrast of comedy and drama is expected. Also classical and modern. Only use native accents if you want to use a dialect. There are a great many actors around from America, Ireland, Scotland, Wales etc. And it is not sensible to put yourself in competition with the real thing.

If you're fortunate enough to work with BBC Radio then again the ability to pick up a script and 'lift' the part off the page is a 'must'. For an afternoon play or a longer work on Radio 3 you will get a script with sufficient time to study your part. Raising your eyes off the script and making contact with the other actors or looking straight into the microphone to express your inner emotions and thoughts are the beauty of radio work and are very satisfying for the actor. Radio is experiencing a renaissance in this new Millennium. Long may it continue.

The spoken word is important and the recording field is vast. There are numerous Talking Books, Shakespearean CDs, language tapes, children's cassettes, all giving opportunities to the vocally well equipped actor.

If you love a particular book and have an ambition to read it and as far as you know it hasn't been recorded recently it is worthwhile doing a bit of research to find out if any of the publishers who have media departments would be interested. They'll probably want a 'star name' but it is worth a go.

Simple voice exercises keep the voice in trim and these should be done gently every day. Don't lose your original accent as it is useful for television drama, soaps etc. but work at Received Pronunciation for the opportunity to work in classical drama. Keep reading and above all enjoy.'

CAROL SCHRODER LLAM is an Examiner for the London Academy of Music and Dramatic Art (LAMDA) and an experienced teacher of drama and performing arts. She is the author of several textbooks.

'This is an imaginative, exciting and well researched collection of scenes. Whilst using some well known sources there is a wealth of material from new writers representing plays that have been performed in a variety of theatres from the fringe to the West End and other countries.

The scenes offer scope to actors of all ages and experience and will equip them with a range of material that will admirably demonstrate their versatility, either for auditions or examinations. Many are taken from plays written since 1985 and this is an essential criteria of the syllabus requirements for the LAMDA medal examinations.

It is always rewarding to discover new material, especially that which will challenge the actor and give pleasure both in the preparation and the performance.'

a word about the speeches

Each of the following speeches has its own introduction, giving the date of the original production – information often required for auditions and drama examinations – a few lines about the play itself, and the scene leading up to the actual speech. Even so, it is important to read the whole play. Not only will you most probably be asked questions such as, 'What happened in the previous scene?' but also the other characters in the play can give you vital information about your character.

At the top left hand corner of each introduction I have, where possible, given the age, or approximate age of the character, and their nationality, and/or the region or area they come from. If a region or nationality is not mentioned then standard English, RP (Received

Pronunciation), or your own voice should be used. When a play is in translation, or is set in another country, only characters foreign to that particular country need to use an accent or dialect. In other words – use your own voice. No funny accents! Here again, reading the whole play should give you a better idea of whether the character is suited to you.

At the back of this book there are an additional ten speeches, briefly outlined, for you to find and research for yourselves. An actress friend of mine who taught for a while at the Royal Academy of Dramatic Art, used to send her students out to find a speech they had never seen before and present it in class the following week. This can be a useful exercise. One day you may have to prepare a very special type of speech at short notice and you don't want to get caught out!

audition speeches
for women

Albertine at 30 – 30

ALBERTINE IN FIVE TIMES MICHEL TREMBLAY

TRANSLATED BY JOHN VAN BUREK AND BILL GLASSCO

First performed in this country at the Donmar Warehouse, London by the Tarragon Theatre, Toronto in 1986.

Albertine is performed by five different actresses at successive ages in the character's life – thirty, forty, fifty, sixty and seventy. All five talk to each other freely and also to **Albertine**'s sister, Madeleine.

Albertine at 30 is recuperating after viciously beating her eleven year old daughter, Thérèse. In this scene she is trying to explain to Madeleine and the other Albertines the rage she feels inside that led her to attack her own child.

Published by Nick Hern Books, London

Albertine at 30

I'm young, I'm strong, I could do so much if it weren't for this rage, gnawing at me . . . Sometimes I think it's all that keeps me alive . . . I'll tell you why I'm here this week, Madeleine, you'll understand . . . You'll understand what I mean by this rage.

(Silence. The other Albertines *and* Madeleine *listen carefully.)*
My child, my own daughter, my Thérèse, who I fight with all the time because we're so alike . . . though I try to bring her up as best I can . . . It's true, you know, I do the best I can . . . I don't know much, but what I do know I try to pass on to my kids . . . though they never listen. Another thing that enrages me . . . Anyway . . . my Thérèse who I always thought was so innocent, with her dolls and those girlfriends she leads around by the nose . . . Believe it or not, she was seeing a man. A man, Madeleine, not some brat her own age who'd be happy to kiss her with her mouth closed, but a grown man! . . . Eleven years old, Madeleine, and he was chasing her like she was a woman! Following her everywhere. And she let him do what he liked, without a word. She knew, and she didn't say a word! . . . She liked it, Madeleine, she told me herself. And that's why I beat her. . . . Naturally I found out by accident. I was lying on the sofa the other day, in the middle of the afternoon . . . I could feel a storm brewing . . . Mother'd been in a rotten mood all day, the kids were driving me nuts . . . Thérèse came to sit on the front balcony with her friend Pierrette.

(Silence.)

They talked about it like it was an everyday thing . . . Pierrette asked Thérèse if she'd seen her 'gent' lately and she said he disappeared the beginning of June. I assumed it was some neighbourhood kid, and I figured: 'Here we go, boy problems. Already.' Then I realized it wasn't that at all. They were talking about him like he was an actor, for God's sake. Comparing him to those movie stars in the magazines . . . They even said he was better looking! I lay there, horrified . . . They had no idea . . . of the danger . . . the danger of men, Madeleine . . . And when Thérèse started talking about the last time she saw him, how he got down on his knees in front of her right on the street and put his head on . . . her belly, I got up, not knowing what I was doing and went out on the balcony . . . and I started to hit her, Madeleine. . . . I didn't know where I was hitting. I just hit her as hard as I could. Thérèse was screaming, Pierrette was crying, the neighbours coming out of their houses . . . and I didn't stop . . . I couldn't. It wasn't just Thérèse I was hitting, it was . . . my whole life . . . I couldn't find the words to explain the danger, so I just hit! *(She turns toward her sister.)* I never told Thérèse much about men 'cause the words would have been filthy. *(Silence.)* If Gabriel hadn't come out and separated us, I would have killed her.

(Madeleine puts her hand on her sister's shoulder who throws herself into her arms.)

I didn't cry, Madeleine. Not once. And I still can't. *(Silence.)* Rage.

Prue – aged 25–30
ANNA'S ROOM ELLEN DRYDEN

First performed at the Birmingham Repertory Studio in 1984.

Anna moves into a flat with her girl friend, **Prue**, to escape from a stifling relationship. In the old attic room that she makes into her study, Anna 'sees' the ghosts of women from the past. Through these ghosts and the continuing visits from her ever faithful boyfriend Simon, **Prue**'s mother and self-seeking brother, Anna reviews her life and what she intends to do with it.

In this scene Anna, Simon and **Prue** have just finished supper. They are relaxed and cheerful. **Prue** comments that baked beans on toast with melted cheese is one of the great experiences of life. Simon tells her to make the most of it. Anna is going macro-biotic and soon the window boxes will be full of bean sprouts and alfalfa.

Published by First Writes Publications, London

Prue

I'm not going to live on health foods. I had enough of that when I was a kid. My mother was obsessional about my teeth and my bowels. They used to laugh at me at school. There was a sweet shop outside my primary school. And everybody tumbled out at half-past three and bought Mars bars and iced lollies and crisps and Kola Kubes and rhubarb and custard sweets. And I wasn't allowed any of them. And when I moaned at my mum that everybody had something nice when they came out of school she brought me a little bag of carrots and raisins . . . and nuts. I could have died. There were some girls in the juniors that saw it and until the day they left they used to put their fingers to their heads like this –

(She puts her fingers like donkey's ears to the side of her head)

– and shout 'Hee Haw.' Poor Mum. *(Sitting back)* Of course I haven't got any fillings *(Mock dramatically)* except on my soul! I never said anything to her though. My brother didn't either. He just organised a protection racket in the playground. Threatened all the little kids with instant death if they didn't pay him a percentage of their sweet money. He was brilliant. He never took more than a penny from any one child. But he'd got about eighteen or nineteen victims so he always ended up richer than anybody. Never gave me any . . .

Oh well, he's changed a bit since then. *(With a grin)* No he hasn't. He's all right though. Anyway the point is, include me out of the lentils. I like real rubbish food . . . I like bacon sandwiches with sliced white bread and brown sauce. Peanut butter with Marmite. Frozen chips. Fish fingers. Spaghetti hoops. Cup cakes. Bright pink blancmanges. Tinned peaches. Jelly that hasn't quite set, swimming with evaporated milk. But my very favourite food of all is corned beef fritters . . .

No. I am a child of my time. Have you ever shelled a pound of peas? All that work and all those maggots crawling about and all those nasty little black bits. You finish up with a teaspoonful of rock hard green pellets, and a great pile of maggoty pods. Because all the best ones have gone to Bird's Eye anyway. I don't believe in leaving anything to nature. My only concession to healthy living is prunes every morning to keep me regular . . . But I do like them as well.

Ruth – mid 30s

BLITHE SPIRIT NOEL COWARD

First produced at the Opera House, Manchester in June 1941 and later that year at the Piccadilly Theatre, London. The action takes place in the living room of Charles Condomine's house in Kent.

Charles Condomine, an author whose first wife, Elvira, died seven years ago has recently married again. He is gathering material for a new book about a homicidal clairvoyant and invites a local medium, Madame Arcati, to conduct a séance at his home in order to learn a few 'tricks of the trade'. However, he gets more than he bargained for when Elvira returns from the 'other side' and proceeds to make life extremely awkward for him. As she is visible and audible only to Charles, he has difficulty convincing his second wife, **Ruth**, that he is neither mad nor drunk. **Ruth** asks Madame Arcati to help them but there is nothing she can do.

In this scene Charles tells **Ruth** they will just have to make the best of the situation. Perhaps if she could be 'a bit more friendly towards Elvira they might all have quite a jolly time.' **Ruth** is by now becoming hysterical and Charles makes matters worse by addressing Elvira as 'darling'.

Published by Samuel French, London

Ruth

Who was that 'darling' addressed to – her or me? . . . *(stamping her foot)*
This is intolerable! . . . *(Furiously)* I've been doing my level best to
control myself ever since yesterday morning, and I'm damned if I'm
going to try any more, the strain is too much. She has the advantage of
being able to say whatever she pleases without me being able to hear
her, but she can hear me all right, can't she, without any modified inter-
preting? . . . you haven't told me once what she really said – you
wouldn't dare. Judging from her photograph she's the type who would
use most unpleasant language. . . . I've been making polite conversation all through dinner last night and breakfast and lunch today – and
it's been a nightmare – and I am not going to do it any more. I don't
like Elvira any more than she likes me, and what's more, I'm certain that
I never could have, dead or alive. If, since her untimely arrival here the
other evening, she had shown the slightest sign of good manners, the
slightest sign of breeding, I might have felt differently towards her, but
all she has done is try to make mischief between us and have private
jokes with you against me. I am now going up to my room and I shall
have my dinner on a tray. You and she can have the house to yourselves
and joke and gossip with each other to your heart's content. *(Spoken in
the doorway)* The first thing in the morning I am going up to London
to interview the Psychical Research Society, and if they fail me I shall go
straight to the Archbishop of Canterbury . . .
  (She exits)

Marie – Belfast, 30s
BOLD GIRLS RONA MUNRO

First performed at the Cumberland Theatre, Strathclyde in 1991.

The play depicts the lives of three women, **Marie**, Cassie and Nora in war-torn Belfast. Although their men have been killed or imprisoned for political activities, life still has to go on.

This scene is set in **Marie**'s kitchen. Here, almost at the beginning of the play, she is preparing bread for the birds as she talks about her brother, Davey and her husband, Michael and his friends.

Published by Hodder & Stoughton, London

Marie

I like the pigeons. I saw a pigeon fly across the sky and when it crossed the clouds it was black but when it flew past the roofs it was white. It could fly as far as it liked but it never went further than Turf Lodge from what I could see. *(Pause)* I used to watch for that bird, the only white bird that wasn't a seagull. *(Pause)* He wasn't even the man they wanted, but they shot him; that made him the man they wanted. *(Pause)* You have to imagine the four of them. All men you'd look at twice one way or another. Michael, my husband, because he had that strong feel to him. You felt it in the back of your neck when he came in a room. People turned to look without knowing why. Davey, my brother now, you'd look again but you'd say, what's that wee boy doing in his daddy's jacket. Nineteen and he looks more like nine, though they've put age in his eyes for him now. He's got old eyes now. Martin, Cassie's brother, you'd look and you'd cross the street in case he caught your eye and decided he didn't like the look of *you*, he's got the kind of eyebrows that chop short conversations, slamming a glower on his face like two fists hitting a table – and Joe, Cassie's husband. You'd look at him to see what the joke was, Joe's always laughing. Joe's always where the crack is. *(Pause)* Davey's in the Kesh. Martin's in the Kesh. Joe's in the Kesh – and Michael is dead. *(Pause)* They didn't really go round together, the four of them, just every odd Saturday they'd be in here playing cards till they were three of them broke and Joe stuffed with beer and winnings. Singing till they were too drunk to remember the words then waking and eating and drinking some more till they were drunk enough to make up their own. Sure it was a party they had. And Davey felt like a man and Martin smiled and Joe sang almost in tune and Michael would tell me he loved me over and over till he'd made a song out of that. *(Pause)* Sometimes he said he loved me when he'd no drink in him at all. Sometimes he even did that.

Beatrice – 20s
THE CLINK STEPHEN JEFFREYS

First produced by Paines Plough at the Theatre Royal, Plymouth in 1990 and set in and around 'The Clink' – a prison in Southwark, London – towards the end of the reign of Elizabeth the First.

Beatrice is Lady in Waiting to Queen Elizabeth. Her father, a privy councillor to the Queen, has arranged for her to marry Martin Gridling, a man she heartily despises. Her maid, Zanda, devises a plot to get rid of Gridling who is a well known 'roarer'. The girls disguise themselves as 'roaring girls' and invite him to a duel at dawn. Beatrice easily wins this duel of words, then takes a pistol from her cloak and shoots him dead. The blame is laid on the innocent Lucius Bodkin who had been persuaded to act as Gridling's second.

In this scene Beatrice, covered in mud, is sitting on the floor of her room while Zanda brushes out her hair. She is in ecstasy over the murder. Zanda says she must conceal her crime for both their sakes, but when her father arrives home she can't wait to tell him how she shot her husband-to-be through the heart with silver bullets.

Published by Nick Hern Books, London

Beatrice

I see his face. A piece of parchment scratched on by a child and left out in the rain. The mud of London's fields spattering his eyes and nose. Mud on my boots. After killing, every action so loud. I tug at a broken nail, the rip of it deafens me. Again and again I feel the jolt of the pistol in my hand. The ease of it. The ecstasy. . . .

(Beatrice stands suddenly. The hairbrush drops to the floor.)

I have snapped a link in the chain of being, a small snip to a link and now the chain is sundered, and what is outside the chain? They told me hell, and they told me falsely. I killed but I am not in the furnace. I am in the thrilling region, the realm of ice where the air is dizzy. . . . I have their secret! I know the secret the men have, that they carry with them, which gives them power! The swords on their hips, their furtive pistols. Killing is exciting, it is power. You knew that from your slave days and yet you kept it from me. . . . Now I am delivered. I am no longer one who waits, looks on and nods agreement. I change the face of the earth. I squeeze a trigger and the world is changed. There is nothing I cannot do! . . . I am a killer. I am one of them. . . . They put a prayer book in my hand and told me God would see my every sin. But I have done the worst, the final sin and am not seen. I have not put myself in prison, I have burst out. You talk of freedom here on earth, freedom of the body, when I speak of my eternal soul. . . .

(Warburton, *her father, comes in. He wears the chain of office.*)
Shot. Through the heart. Silver bullets. In the mud beyond Edgware. . . . I have the pistol here. And here the murderer's hand. . . . Father, I have not thanked you for my education. . . . Not for the Latin and Greek whipped into me, but for your education in the art of politic murder. For did you not show me the way with friend Frobisher, did you not send the Bishop and Lord Davenport to the axe. But there is a fault I find in my killing education, that I must go to finishing school at the feet of our slave. You taught me only the grammar and syntax of murder, but Zanda rendered me the gift of tongues – . . . she put the pistol in my hand and gave me the trigger lesson. I shot the man you wanted for my husband and now I stand forever free. . . . I am let loose for ever. . . .

(She threatens them with the pistol.)
I cannot be confined within my prayer book room. I am now out among the world. There is no chain you can devise that will ever drag me back. I was never innocent. I watched the worms eating at the stair and, in my secret thoughts, considered them good. But now I take a hatchet to the banisters and smile.

(Beatrice *goes.*)

Zanda – originally from Morocco, 20s
THE CLINK STEPHEN JEFFREYS

First produced by Paines Plough at the Theatre Royal, Plymouth in 1990 and set in and around 'The Clink' – a prison in Southwark, London – towards the end of the reign of Elizabeth the First.

Zanda is a slave shipped over from Morocco and bought by privy councillor Warburton to look after his daughter, Beatrice, who is Lady in Waiting to the Queen. Warburton has arranged for his daughter to marry Martin Gridling, a man she heartily despises. **Zanda** devises a plot to get rid of him. Gridling is a well known 'roarer' and the girls disguise themselves as 'roaring girls' and invite him to a duel. Beatrice easily wins this duel of words, then takes a pistol from her cloak and shoots Gridling dead. The blame is laid on the innocent Lucius Bodkin who had been persuaded to act as Gridling's second.

In this scene Beatrice, covered in mud, is musing happily over the murder she has just committed. **Zanda** tries to persuade her to come to bed. They need sleep. The murder must be concealed from her father at all costs and tomorrow they must act their innocence.

Published by Nick Hern Books, London

Zanda

My lady. Will you come to bed? It is time. . . . We will act the perfect maid and lady and follow daily customs. Your father must harbour no suspicion against us. I will brush your hair and soothe you, then you'll sleep. . . . Tomorrow we will fetch water to wash it. Now sit. . . . You are the mistress in the house, but I am Queen in the streets and we have brought the street stink here into your chambers. You do not know what musks and mists can cover murder but I do and you will swallow my prescription. Now sit.

(Beatrice *sits on the floor, but not where* Zanda *has indicated.*
Zanda *goes to her and brushes.*)

When I was a slave to the Spaniards, I was their thing to use as they wished. I fetched for them, skivvied. They took me, sleeping, in sickness, they didn't care. One was the ship's doctor. He grabbed me, sudden while I slept upon the deck. I turned and fisted him, he fell, heavy, his head striking a cannon. Dead. I held his body up and nailed it to the mast. The crew looked on. They never troubled me again. I said: 'Now I am your doctor.' I had broken the chain. . . . As you have broken yours. . . . You have freed yourself. . . . You wait. You live from day to day. You relish the snapping of your chain. . . . I meant the chain that bound you to your father. . . . You must not trumpet out this murder. Your father will be high in anger at this death and you must play bereavement to the hilt. . . . The Queen grows sicker. This is the report from every stair and corridor. When she is dead, your power in the court is gone. All you can ever be is a drain on your father's exchequer or a quim for trading on the market. You have 'scaped one husband, you cannot 'scape them all. . . .

(Zanda *seizes* Beatrice.)

You and I have been as sisters! We have brought the two halves of the globe together and made a safe cocoon to live in, an egg where we have dwelt in safety from the world of men. The shell is shattered now. We must stand together. Without me you will have no access to the world of pleasure and die a country death with a fat husband. Without you I have no privilege and cannot be protected from the curs who call me blackamoor and spit upon my skin. . . . You must conceal this murder. If you broadcast it abroad, my complicity will be much blamed. . . . Your guilt, once known will be laden at my door.

Margo Boye-Anawoma – (a lawyer)
Doreen Lawrence – black, early middle-age

THE COLOUR OF JUSTICE BASED ON THE TRANSCRIPTS OF
THE STEPHEN LAWRENCE INQUIRY
EDITED BY RICHARD NORTON-TAYLOR

First performed at the Tricycle Theatre in January, 1999 and later transferred to the Victoria Palace, London.

This is a dramatic reconstruction of the hearings which erupted into national outrage when black teenager, Stephen Lawrence was stabbed to death by a gang of white youths, and the police investigation failed to provide sufficient evidence to convict.

In this extract lawyer **Margo Boye-Anawoma** continues to read **Doreen Lawrence**'s statement at the Inquiry. **Doreen**, Stephen's mother, is sitting next to her throughout the hearing. The statement describes her frustrated attempts to obtain justice for her son leading up to the Lawrences' decision to begin a private prosecution. This extract could also be played as **Doreen Lawrence** herself making her statement.

Published by Oberon Books, London

Boye-Anawoma

I am going to carry on reading Mrs Lawrence's statement.

(Reads statement.)

'The police were not interested in keeping us informed about the investigation. We were simply regarded as irritants.

'It was also claimed that the police found dealing with our solicitor a hindrance. Basically, we were seen as gullible simpletons. This is best shown by Ilsley's comment that I had obviously been primed to ask questions. Presumably, there is no possibility of me being an intelligent, black woman with thoughts of her own who is able to ask questions for herself. We were patronised and we were fobbed off. As the meetings went on, I got more and more angry. I thought that the purpose of the meetings was to give us progress reports, but what actually happened was that they would effectively say: stop questioning us. We are doing everything. That simply was not true, and it led me to believe then and now that they were protecting the suspects.

'The second investigation started with meeting Commissioner Condon in April 1994. We discussed the Barker review, and that was the first time we met Ian Johnston. We were still kept in the dark about some things in the second investigation. We weren't told exactly what was happening, but we heard rumours that things had gone wrong with the first investigation, and I think there was some cover-up about what was going on. It was then decided that the Crown Prosecution Service wouldn't take matters further. I felt we had no choice but to take a private prosecution, and I don't believe they would have been acquitted if we could have presented everything to the jury. On the first day at the Old Bailey I was extremely optimistic, but from the minute the judge opened his mouth, my hopes were dashed. It was clear from the outset he had come with the intention of not letting the matter proceed further. The judge instructed them to return a verdict of not guilty. When he told them that there was no alternative they actually went outside to consider it and then came back in. They didn't want to do it.

'. . . At the beginning the Kent Police Complaints Authority Report was saying that the police officers were not racist in their attitude. If it wasn't racism what was it? Incompetence? Corruption? . . .

'I would like Stephen to be remembered as a young man who had a future. He was well loved and had he been given the chance to survive maybe he would have been the one to bridge the gap between black and white; he just saw people as people.' *(Statement ends.)*

Mona – Texan, 17

COME BACK TO THE FIVE & DIME, JIMMY DEAN, JIMMY DEAN ED GRACZYK

First produced at the Martin Beck Theatre, New York in 1982. This play is set in a 'Five-and-Dime' in McCarthy – a small town in West Texas. On the walls are framed pictures of James Dean and a crudely painted sign reads, 'The 20th Anniversary Reunion of the Disciples of James Dean September 30th 1955 – September 10th 1975'.

The Disciples are gathered together for their twentieth reunion. They are by now middle-aged women who were teenagers when James Dean filmed *Giant* two decades ago in nearby Marfa. **Mona** was an extra on the film and has a child who she insists was fathered by James Dean and is the 'Jimmy Dean' of the title. The ladies reminisce in flashbacks to their youth. And **Mona** is persuaded to tell them, yet again, how she met James Dean and was chosen to play in the film.

In this scene the seventeen year old **Mona** tells her story.

Published by Samuel French, London

Mona

There were nearly four thousand . . . people in that small town when we got there. All the rooms in the Paisano Hotel were filled-up, so Joe an' I had to sleep in the Buick along the side of the road. . . . Next mornin' . . . after I had washed up in the sink of the gas station across the road, nearly rubbin' my skin off with Boraxo an' paper towels . . . I was sittin' in the back seat of the Buick pourin' lilac perfume all over to get rid of the smell of the Boraxo, when I saw 'him' walkin' down the road, right towards me . . . an' he stopped right next to the car, lookin' in his pocket for somethin'. There was a cigarette danglin' from out of the corner of his mouth, so I took a chance that a match was what he was huntin' for and I leaned out the car window an' says . . . 'I've got a match, if that's what you're needin'.' He sort of smiled an' took the matches just like he had been livin' in Texas all his life . . . When he lit his cigarette and I looked up into them deep-set, sky-blue eyes . . . I could see myself, clear as lookin' in a mirror. It was at that very moment I knew somethin' was gonna happen to change my whole life. . . .

Later on at the place where they were pickin' people to be in the movie . . . an' they picked me . . . me, out of all them hundreds of others . . . I knew for certain!

They were lookin' for types. (*To* Joe) You just weren't the right type, that's all. . . .

Elizabeth Taylor's head keeps gettin' in the way . . . but, I'm there, mostly behin' her left ear in that scene where she first arrives from her papa's plantation in Virginia . . . an' they have that big barbecue picnic scene. She gets real hot an' starts to faint, grabbin' onto the branch of a mesquite tree for support . . . right as the camera comes close to her at that point . . . you can see me peekin' out from behin' her left ear.

Joe, if you aren't interested in listenin' . . . you can leave. *[She goes on building to a desperate frenzy.]* That night I laid there in the back seat of the Buick and kept thinkin' about how I was chosen above all them thousands of others . . . starin' out the window at the millions of stars an' the outline of that beautiful house way off in the distance. Suddenly, one of those stars exploded, burst away from all the millions of others an' fell from the sky . . . landin' right behin' the house . . . behin' the front of Reata. I leaned over the seat to point it out to Joe, but he had tramped off somewhere, all mad 'cause he wasn't chosen, too. . . .

I pulled my blanket aroun' my shoulders an' started to walk to where the star had fallen to earth. I walked past the front gate down the road to the house. It was so quiet and still . . . the only sound was comin' from a far away train, blowin' its whistle an' chuggin' off into the night. When I got to the front porch, this voice comin' outta nowhere says, 'Isn't it a little late to be callin' on your neighbours?' It was him. I knew it. I knew it the first minute I heard his voice. Then he said, 'Don't just stand there bein' unfriendly. Come on up on the porch an' sit a spell.' As I moved up the stairs, I reminded him that I was the one who gave him a match that mornin' . . . an he thanked me again. We spent that whole entire night together . . . until the sun started to peek out from over the edge of the earth, turnin' the sky into the brightest red I ever saw. . . . *[Sharply to* Joe*]* We walked together to the gate an' he thanked me for sharin' the night with him an' then we both walked away in separate directions.

Eleonora – young
EASTER AUGUST STRINDBERG
TRANSLATED BY PETER WATTS

First performed at the Intima Teatern, Stockholm in 1901 and in Katie Mitchell's production for the Royal Shakespeare Company in The Pit at the Barbican in 1995, it is set in the small provincial town of Lund over Easter.

Eleonora is a young sensitive girl who has just returned from the Asylum, where she was being treated for a mental breakdown. Her father is serving a prison sentence for embezzlement and the family are haunted by creditors.

In this scene she is talking to Benjamin – a young schoolboy who is staying with them and taking private tuition with her brother. She describes how on her way back from the Asylum she broke into a flower shop that was closed for Confirmation Day and took a daffodil in a pot as a present for her brother, leaving a krona and her card on the counter.

Published by Penguin Classics, London

Eleonora

Shall I tell you about the flowers? Do you know that when I was ill, they made me take a drug made out of henbane which has the power of turning your eyes into magnifying-glasses – Now, belladonna makes you see everything smaller. Anyhow, now I can see much farther than anyone else – I can even see the stars in broad daylight. . . . The stars are always there. I'm facing north now, and I can see Cassiopeia like a great 'W' in the Milky Way. Can you see it? . . . Make a note of that, then: some people can see things that others can't – so don't be too sure of your own eyes. Now I'll tell you about this flower on the table; it's a daffodil, and they come from Switzerland. It has sucked the sunlight into its cup – that's what makes it so yellow, and that's how it can soothe pain. I saw it as I passed a flower-shop just now, and I wanted it for a present for my brother Elis, but when I tried to get in, I found the door was locked, because it's Confirmation Day. I simply had to have the flower, though, so I took out my keys and tried them, and – would you believe it? – my latch-key fitted, so I went in. Now, you know about the silent language of flowers? Well, every scent expresses a whole multitude of thoughts, and all those thoughts came flooding in on me; so with my magnifying eye, I looked into their laboratories where no one has ever seen before, and they told me about the pain that the clumsy gardener had caused them – I won't call him cruel, because he was only thought-less. And then I left a krona on the counter, with my card, and I took the flower and went.

Tamara – 29
THE EDITING PROCESS MEREDITH OAKES

First performed at the Royal Court Theatre, London in 1994 and set in a London publishing company in the 1990's.

In publicity beware of everyone, especially your friends. Swept by the cold winds of change toward a risky corporate future, the editorial staff of *Footnotes in History* engage in a desperate battle for survival. **Tamara del Fuego** has been brought in by Lionel, the General Manager of the parent publishing company, to transform the company's fortunes with a new corporate image. She has already vastly overspent her budget and has become involved with Ted, the assistant editor. Together they were responsible for a tin of oysters being spilt over the computer while they were having sex in the photocopying room.

In this scene she meets Eleanor walking along the corridor towards her. Eleanor has only just joined the company as a trainee, but **Tamara** knows it is important to keep in with her as her uncle is on the Board.

Published by Oberon Books, London

Tamara

My computer's down, Eleanor. . . . Do you want to see your new letter-head? It's gorg. *(Eleanor looks)* Go on, tell me you love it, it's a mock-up obviously, the editor's name goes there, we can put that in later in order to avoid any uncertainty. . . . Isn't it beautiful. . . . That's exactly what I was aiming for, timeless is the next big thing. What's your game plan, Eleanor? When I was your age I had the next ten years mapped out. Well I still am your age. . . . Sometimes I think what I do is actually therapy, you know? Helping companies through a crisis of identity? Because there's no such thing as a bad company. We're talking a confused company, with myself as the medium through which this company can be released. The company talks to me and I listen. I help the company to express what was previously perhaps too obvious for anyone to mention. When I encourage a company to create its new corporate image, that's like a rite of passage for that company, it achieves a deeper awareness of what it wants to project, and I give it the tools it needs to define itself. So it becomes a sort of celebration, a coming of age or a wedding feast, where money should be no object. . . . Anyway Lionel told this company I'd be mega. They're not expecting the Seven Wise Virgins. Hostess to a concept is what I am. Well of course the company's given me a budget and I've totally overspent it, and I think everyone should feel they've had a wonderful blow-out and that it's a really special time. I mean I hope your uncle will understand. Perhaps you could have a talk with him. If you're interested, the girl that does my office is having a baby and I'm going to have to replace her, I didn't realize I was harbouring a breeder, I don't pay much but it isn't about pay, ultimately, is it. . . . Don't think your uncle's going to do anything for you, the owner only uses him for getting into clubs. . . . Don't stay too long, this company's dodgier than eggs.

Des-Neiges – Glaswegian, middle-aged

THE GUID SISTERS MICHEL TREMBLAY

A TRANSLATION OF *LES BELLES-SOEURS* BY BILL FINDLAY AND
MARTIN BOWMAN

Les Belles-Soeurs was first performed in Montreal in 1968 and it's
Scots version, *The Guid Sisters* was seen in Glasgow in 1989.

The play is set in the kitchen of a tenement flat where Germaine
has won a million premium stamps. These have to be pasted into
book before they can be exchanged for goods, and so she has invited
her friends and female relatives to a stamp-sticking party. They are
jealous of her good fortune and moan about their less fortunate
lives. One by one, as they are chatting away they steal the books of
stamps, until Germaine notices they are missing and makes them
all turn out their bags.

Throughout the action the women are singled out by a spotlight
as they reveal their innermost thoughts. **Des-Neiges** has been
telling the others a dirty joke. Gabrielle remarks that she gets all
her jokes from a travelling salesman with whom she is more than
'friendly'. **Des-Neiges** protests that there is nothing in their relationship and that she is 'a respectable woman an a good Catholic'. The
spotlight is now turned on **Des-Neiges**.

Published by Nick Hern Books, London

(Spotlight on Des-Neiges.*)*
Des-Neiges

The first time I seen him I thought he was ugly. At least, I didnae think he was guid-looking tae start wi. When I opened the door he took off his hat an said tae me, 'Would the lady of the house be interested in buying some brushes?' I shut the door in his face. I never allows a man intae ma hoose. Ye never know what might happen . . . The only one 'at gets in is the paper boy. He's still owre young tae get any funny ideas. Anyhows, a month later back he came wi his brushes. It was bucketin ootside so I let him stand in the lobby. Once he was in the hoose, I started tae get jittery, but I tellt masel he didnae look the dangerous type, even if he wasnae very bonny tae look at . . . But he ayeways looks that smart. No a hair oot ae place. Like a real gentleman. And he's ayeways that polite. Well, he selled me a couple ae brushes an then he showed me his catalogue. There was somethin 'at I wanted but he didnae have it wi him so he said I could order it. Ever since then, he's come back once a month. Sometimes I dinnae buy anythin. But he jist comes in an we blether for a wee while. He's an awful nice man . . . I think . . . I really think I'm in love wi him . . . I know it's daft . . . I only see him once a month . . . But it's that nice when we're thegither. I'm that happy when he comes. I've never felt like this afore. It's the first time it's happened tae me. For usual men've never paid me any notice. I've aye been . . . on the shelf, so tae speak. He tells me all aboot his trips, an all kinna stories an jokes. Sometimes his jokes are a wee bit near the bone, but they're that funny! I don't know why, but I've always liked jokes that are a wee bit dirty. It's good for ye, tae, for tae tell dirty jokes noo an again. Mind you, no all his jokes are dirty. Lots ae them are clean. An it's only jist recent he's started tellin me the dirty ones. Sometimes they're that dirty I blush red as a beetroot. The last time he tellt me one he took ma hand cause I blushed. Well, I vernear died. Ma insides went all funny when he put his big hand on mines. I need him sae much! I don't want him tae go away! Sometimes, jist noo an again, I dream aboot him. I dream . . . that we're married. I need him tae come back an see me. He's the first man 'at's ever paid me any notice. I don't want tae lose him! I dinnae want tae lose him! If he goes away, I'll be left on ma own again, and I need . . . somedy tae love . . . *(She lowers her eyes and murmurs)* I need a man.
  (The lights come back on)

Lise – Glaswegian, young
THE GUID SISTERS MICHEL TREMBLAY
A TRANSLATION OF *LES BELLES-SOEURS* BY BILL FINDLAY AND MARTIN BOWMAN

Les Belles-Soeurs was first performed in Montreal in 1968 and its Scots version, *The Guid Sisters* was seen in Glasgow in 1989.

The play is set in the kitchen of a tenement flat where Germaine has won a million premium stamps. These have to be pasted into books before they can be exchanged for goods, and so she has invited her friends and female relatives to a stamp-sticking party. They are jealous of her good fortune and moan to each other about their less fortunate lives. One by one they steal the books of stamps until Germaine notices that they are missing and insists that they all turn out their bags. Throughout the action the women are singled out by a spotlight as they reveal their innermost thoughts.

Lise has been brought along to the party by Germaine's daughter, Linda. They are both standing in the spotlight, isolated from the older women, as **Lise** announces that she is pregnant. They are joined by Pierrette who has overhead the conversation and suggests an abortion. Linda strongly disapproves – 'It's criminal!'

Published by Nick Hern Books, London

Lise

What else would ye have me dae? What choice have I got? It's the only way oot. I don't want the wean. Look what happened tae Manon Belair. She was in the same position an noo her life's wasted cause she's lumbered wi that kid. . . . [The father?] Ye know fine he dropped us. He beat it soon's he found oot. Naebody seems tae know where he's went. When I think ae the promises he made us. How happy we were gaunnae be thegither, an how he was makin money hand-owre-fist. Eejit that I am. I taen it all in. It was presents here, presents there . . . there was nae end tae them. Aw, it was nice enough at the time . . . in fact, it was really nice . . . But bugger it, then this had tae happen. I jist knew it would. I've never been gien a break. Never. Why is it me ayeways lands heidfirst in the shite when all I want tae dae is climb oot ae it? I'm bloody well sick ae workin behind the counter in that shop. I want tae dae somethin wi ma life. D'ye understand? I want tae get somewhere. I want a car, a nice flat, some nice claes. Christ knows, aboot all I've got tae put on ma back are shop overalls. I've aye been hard up . . . aye had tae scrimp'n scrape . . . But I'm damn sure I'm no gaunnae go on like this. I don't want tae be a naebody any more. I've had enough ae bein poor. I'm gaunnae make sure things gets better. I was mebbe born at the bottom ae the pile but I'm gaunnae climb tae the top. I came intae this world bi the back door but by Christ I'm gaunnae go oot bi the front. An ye can take it fae me that nothin's gaunnae get in ma way. Nothin. You wait, Linda. Jist you wait. You'll see I'm no kiddin. In two three years you'll see that Lise Paquette's become a somebody. Jist you watch, she'll be rollin in it then. . . . That's what I'm tryin tae tell ye. I've made a mistake an I want tae put it right. After that I'm gaunnae make a new start. You understand what I'm saying, Pierrette, don't ye?

Pierrette – Glaswegian, 30

THE GUID SISTERS MICHEL TREMBLAY

A TRANSLATION OF *LES BELLES-SOEURS* BY BILL FINDLAY AND MARTIN BOWMAN

Les Belles-Soeurs was first performed in Montreal in 1968 and its Scots version, *The Guid Sisters* was seen in Glasgow in 1989.

The play is set in the kitchen of a tenement flat where Germaine has won a million premium stamps. These have to be pasted into books before they can be exchanged for goods, and so she has invited her friends and female relatives to a stamp-sticking party. They are jealous of her good fortune and moan to each other about their less fortunate lives. One by one they steal the books of stamps until Germaine notices that they are missing and insists that they all turn out their bags. Throughout the action the women are singled out by a spotlight as they reveal their innermost thoughts.

Pierrette is Germaine's younger sister and has arrived at the party uninvited. Germaine wants nothing to do with her, describing her as 'a wee hure'.

In this sene the spotlight is turned on **Pierette**. She has just been advising young Lise about having an abortion and during the last part of this speech Lise is repeating over and over, 'Oh, Sweet Jesus, I'm feart' – finally throwing herself into **Pierrette**'s arms.

Published by Nick Hern Books, London

Pierrette

When I left hame I was that in love ma heid was back tae front. I could-nae see straight. I'd eyes for naebody but Johnny. Naebody else counted. That bastard made me squander ten years ae ma life. Here I am, only thirty year ae age, an I feels like sixty. The things that chancer got me tae dae for him. I was aye taen in by his patter, eejit that I am. Ten years I knocked ma guts oot in his Club for him. I was smashin lookin then. I drew his customers in an that kept him sweet as long as it lasted. But as for that bastard noo, I've had ma full. I'm sick-scunnert . . . Deid-done cawin ma pan oot, an for what? All I feel fit for is jumpin off a bridge. It's jist the drink that keeps me gaun. I've been on the bottle solid since last Friday past. And that poor Lise thinks she's all washed up just cause she's pregnant! Christ Almighty, she's young yet! I'm gaunnae gie her ma doctor's name'n address . . . He'll see her right. She can make a new start. No me, though. If ye've been at it for ten year, ye're owre the hill. A has-been. But how could I even begin tae explain that tae ma sisters? They'd never understand. No in a month ae Sundays. I don't know what I'm gaunnae dae noo. What'm I tae dae?

He chucked me oot, jist like that! 'It's all finished,' he said. 'You're nae more use tae me. You're too auld noo an past your best. So ye can pack your bags an beat it. You're no wanted.' The heartless gett! He didnae leave me wi a cent! Not a cent! The bastard! After all that I did for him owre the past ten year! Ten year for sweet bugger-all! If that wouldnae make ye want tae dae away wi yoursel, what would? What'm I tae dae? Eh, jist what? Stand at the back ae a counter all day like Lise? Become a shop-assistant? No thank you! Nae danger! That's awright for young bit lassies an auld women, but no for me. What'm I tae dae? I've jist nae idea. I've got tae put a face on it here. I cannae tell the truth tae Linda and Lise or I'm all washed up. *(Silence.)* Aye, well . . . there's nothin left but the drink noo . . . Guid job I like the stuff *(To Lise, laughing)* Aye, aye. Everything'll be jist fine, hen. You'll see. Everything'll be okay . . .

Christine – Midlands, late 30s
HARVEST ELLEN DRYDEN

First performed at the Birmingham Repertory Studio Theatre in October 1980 and subsequently at the Ambassador's Theatre, London in 1981. It was published in 1996.

The play is set in a small, working-class Midlands village, in a family living within the Methodist church. This is emphasised by the set, which is quickly transformed from chapel into family sitting room. It tells the story of Ted's decision to give up his attempt to get an English degree as a mature student and his sister Marian's efforts to claim her brother for the intellectually liberated world she has moved into.

The opening scene is the funeral service for Marian's granddad, Harry Fenton and changes into the living room where Marian and her sister-in-law, **Christine**, are preparing sandwiches for Harry's friends and relations. **Christine** is a generous hard-working woman with a deep vein of pessimism which makes her suspicious of everything. She communicates almost the whole time by grumbling and attacking. She has a 'posh' Midlands accent.

Published by First Writes Publications, London

Christine

(Inspecting a sandwich)
This ham's all fat! *(She pulls a disgusted face)* Oh, that's nice, isn't it. I told Mom to leave it to me but she wouldn't be said. I expect it's come from the Shop. I think it's disgusting. That great big ham stands there on that cracked plate week in, week out, on the counter – flies buzzing all over it. And Mrs Hollins picks up any old knife to cut it. She can't see beyond her nose-end now, you know. She's always cutting herself. She's never got less than two dirty old plasters on her fingers. Handling food! Then she'll go and serve somebody paraffin and go back to cutting cheese without so much as wiping her fingers. She boils those hams in that old copper, you know, and I wouldn't like to swear that *his* overalls don't go in of a Monday! I told Mom if she wanted ham I could get her some nice wrapped from Marks and Spencers. . . . It would have been the proper shape for sandwiches as well. Look at this!
(She holds out a sandwich with misshapen bits of ham in it)
I mean, when you go to a funeral you don't want to pick up a ham sandwich with bumps in it! I shan't know where to put myself handing these round. . . . *(Tartly)* Well, I'm not proposing to do it on my own. *(Inspecting the rest of the sandwiches)* At least the cheese are a decent shape! But that's only because it's cheese slices – I told her not to get cheese slices. People don't like them. They're all right for convenience, but I don't think they're right for this sort of occasion. I mean it's just not funny, is it? I don't care for Mr Halpern personally but he did go to Cambridge University and I'm sure he'll expect something a bit better than this. . . . I didn't think much of the service anyway. Sitting there like idiots in complete silence. I think he could have thought up *something* a bit nice to say about Granddad. . . . It's his job. Oh my goodness! Don't have a jam tart, Marian. There aren't enough to go round. There's six of this and six of that. Oh, if I'd known what she was up to! . . . *(Vehemently)* You can't get her to do anything properly. You'd think it was still wartime. . . .

Oh! I don't know where Ted's got to. They should be here by now. It's Mrs Ransome keeping them talking, I bet. Getting her pound of flesh – I knew it was a mistake not to invite her to the funeral. She always turns nasty if she doesn't get asked to things.

Susanna – Warwickshire, late 20s
THE HERBAL BED PETER WHELAN

First performed by the Royal Shakespeare Company at The Other Place, Stratford-upon-Avon in 1996 and later at the Barbican Theatre, London. It transferred to the Duchess Theatre, London in 1997.

The play is based on events that took place in the summer of 1613, when William Shakespeare's daughter, **Susanna**, married to John Hall, a respected physician of Stratford, was publicly accused by her husband's young apprentice of having a sexual liasion with Ralph, a family friend.

In this scene, **Susanna** tells Ralph that John has guessed at their relationship, but does not want the truth acknowledged, even to himself, as this could damage his practice.

Published by Josef Weinberger Plays, London

Susanna

He knows already. . . . He's guessed. . . . It's in his look . . . his tone. It's in everything he doesn't say. . . . He knows and mustn't know. He wants our silence. . . . Honesty is not one thing! Love is not one thing . . . nor loyalty . . . he is loyal to his practice and his patients. He's honest in that. And that is his love. And I come second . . . which I accept . . . oh yes! I've seen the terror in the faces of the sick . . . how they reach out to him, their only hope. I can't put myself before that and don't expect him to. So . . . he wants our silence because, if we speak, all that would be shattered like glass . . . Lady Haines would shun him, Lady Rainsford and Underhill . . . the Earl of Northampton . . . and the rest . . . . . . We need the fees of the better off so he can treat the poor. . . . You can't believe that, even in the case of his practice, he would put anything before God himself! That depends what you mean by God himself. If God himself wants the sick to die in pain. If God himself wants plagues and pestilence. If God himself tears children from their parents with their lives unlived . . . as yours were . . . was that God himself? . . . You honour him! . . . How can you honour him by destroying his work? It's only a matter of what you leave out. You came back to tell me that supper was cancelled. I was working in the dispensary. It took a few minutes to tell me. Hester arrived as you were going. . . . If it were left to me I'd leave it. Let it drop. Soon forgotten. Women are slandered every day . . . they're slandered by the hour! Not so much spoken . . . I could walk through Stratford market and be called a whore fifty times over . . . not in words . . . in looks . . . in sneers and nudges. You put on armour against it as a girl and try to wear it lightly. I'm sure worse things have been said. But we must fight it . . . not for ourselves . . . not even for him . . . but for those he might save.

(As she looks across the garden she sees Elizabeth at the cottage.)
There's Bess . . . playing in the grass. (She waves to her.) What a long road we travel . . .

Ruta Skadi – a witch

HIS DARK MATERIALS PHILIP PULLMAN

ADAPTED FOR STAGE BY NICHOLAS WRIGHT

Adapted from Philip Pullman's three novels into two full length plays *His Dark Materials* was first performed on the Olivier stage at the Royal National Theatre, London in December 2003.

This is an epic tale that spreads itself across time and into strange worlds, old and new. At the centre is Lyra, described as a child with a destiny, who unknown to herself has it in her power to bring about the annihilation of death and the triumph of the mysterious 'dust'. She is accompanied on her quest by her friend, Will and together they set out to rescue young Roger from the child-snatching 'Gobblers' and Lyra's father, Lord Asriel from the clutches of 'The Authority'. On the way they encounter the frightening 'Cliff-Ghasts', 'Armoured Bears' and the 'Witch Clan' of the Arctic.

In this scene, set in the desolate wastes of Lapland, the witch, Serafina is addressing an Assembly of Witches. The meeting is in uproar. Serafina explains that the prophecy has begun. The child Lyra is lost in a maze of worlds and the aeronaut, Lee Scoresby is there to help them find her. One of the witches protests that they don't need help from a short-lived mortal. Then **Ruta Skadi**, Queen of the Latvian Clan steps forward to speak.

Published by Nick Hern Books, London

Ruta Skadi

Let me speak! . . . Serafina Pekkala, to hear you talk, anyone would think that destiny was a poor weak thing that couldn't manage without our help. You're wrong. It's bigger than us. It knows what it's doing. If the child of the prophecy has gone wandering through the worlds, then there's a reason for that, and every mile we fly going after her is a mile in the wrong direction. There's a war approaching! Lord Asriel's gone to kill the Authority. There'll be blood and swords and thunder in heaven like's never been heard since the proudest of all the angels was cast down into blackness. We're *in* this war already, hate it or love it, and I say, let's love it, let's relish and joy in the bloodshed, and it makes no difference what strange allies we find for ourselves, as long as we know our enemy. That's the Church. As long as it's been on this earth, it's suppressed and persecuted everything good about human nature. When it can't suppress it, it cuts it out. They cut the souls out of the children at Bolvangar. They cut out the sexual organs of boys and girls. They burn witches! Yes, sisters! Witches like us!

(A chorus of disgust and anger.)

All to ravage the joy of life, in the name of that monster, that tyrant, the Authority. If the Church is on one side, then we witches have got to be on the other. So let's join together to fight for Lord Asriel. And let Lyra look after herself!

Mabel Chiltern – aged 18–20

AN IDEAL HUSBAND OSCAR WILDE

First performed at the Haymarket Theatre in 1895.

Mabel Chiltern is the young sister of Sir Robert Chiltern – the 'Ideal Husband' of the title. She is described as 'a perfect example of the English type of prettiness . . . She has the fascinating tyranny of youth, and the astonishing courage of innocence . . . '

In this scene, set in the morning room of Sir Robert's house, **Mabel** is complaining to her sister-in-law, Lady Chiltern, about the behaviour of one of her more ardent suitors, Tommy Trafford – Sir Robert's private secretary.

Published by A & C Black Publishers Limited, London

Mabel Chiltern

Gertrude, I wish you would speak to Tommy Trafford. . . .

Well, Tommy has proposed to me again. Tommy really does nothing but propose to me. He proposed to me last night in the music-room, when I was quite unprotected, as there was an elaborate trio going on. I didn't dare to make the smallest repartee, I need hardly tell you. If I had, it would have stopped the music at once. Musical people are so absurdly unreasonable. They always want one to be perfectly dumb at the very moment when one is longing to be absolutely deaf. Then he proposed to me in broad daylight this morning, in front of that dreadful statue of Achilles. Really, the things that go on in front of that work of art are quite appalling. The police should interfere. At luncheon I saw by the glare in his eye that he was going to propose again, and I just managed to check him in time by assuring him that I was a bimetallist. Fortunately I don't know what bimetallism means. And I don't believe anybody else does either. But the observation crushed Tommy for ten minutes. He looked quite shocked. And then Tommy is so annoying in the way he proposes. If he proposed at the top of his voice, I should not mind so much. That might produce some effect on the public. But he does it in a horrid confidential way. When Tommy wants to be romantic he talks to one just like a doctor. 1 am very fond of Tommy, but his methods of proposing are quite out of date.

I wish Gertrude, you would speak to him, and tell him that once a week is quite often enough to propose to anyone, and that it should always be done in a manner that attracts some attention. . . .

I must go round now and rehearse at Lady Basildon's. You remember we are having *tableaux*, don't you? The Triumph of something, I don't know what! I hope it will be triumph of me. Only triumph I am really interested in at present. *(Kisses* Lady Chiltern *and goes out, then comes running back)* Oh, Gertrude, do you know who is coming to see you? That dreadful Mrs Cheveley, in a most lovely gown. Did you ask her? . . .

I assure you she is coming upstairs, as large as life and not nearly so natural.

Steph – Northern, 20s
INDIAN SUMMER LUCY MAURICE

First presented by Eva Productions at the Upstairs at the Landor Theatre in 1996, it is set in a British Rail café on a Sunday night.

There are two girls working at the counter, **Steph** and Laura. **Steph** is married with a boy, Tom, to bring up and looks forward to coming out in the evening. Laura is younger and anxious to move on. Throughout the action they carry out their work routine, stopping only to take on the characters of the various customers that come into the café for a coffee and a bit of a chat.

In this scene **Steph** is going from table to table filling up pepper and salt pots, while Laura is unpacking bread and moaning about the job and the 'weirdos' they meet. **Steph** laughs to herself. She loves the 'weirdos' and likes working in the café.

Published by First Writes Publications, London

Steph

I call them pieces of pie . . . your weirdos. I love them! All little bits of pie, making up one great big pie! *(She laughs to herself.)* . . . I like it here, all the comings and goings. Makes me feel central with everyone else around me. *(Pause.)* I came into this station you know, when we moved down here. I was a comer and goer . . . a piece of pie! Except I only came and I haven't gone yet. Funny I end up working here . . . it's funny that! . . . *(Pause)* Oh Laura, Friday . . . oh! – Tom had a fall at school, bumped his head! . . . I was so worried. It hurts you in here *(Tapping her heart.)* when they hurt themselves. It's worse than doing it yourself. I wasn't even there. . . . He's all right now. He had mild concussion though. . . . You know, when I was Tom's age at school, I wanted to be the angel Gabriel in the Nativity, but I were never allowed! I had to be a shepherd and stuff a cuddly toy under me arm and pretend it were a lamb! Oh, but I wanted to be that angel! Wear a big white sheet and a bit of tinsel in your hair! You know, the angel got all the attention and the shepherds were just left milling around. I bumped my head one year and they didn't notice, till I fell over and knocked Mary off her cuddly donkey and she started crying and I got the blame! I wasn't allowed to be a shepherd again the next year. They said I wasn't meek and humble enough! So they made me be Joseph, cos I were the tallest in class. I hope my Tom gets to play Gabriel . . . but if he takes after me he'll get stuck at the back somewhere . . . Strange I remember all that. Sticks in your mind, don't it?

Evelyn – 50s

KINDERTRANSPORT DIANE SAMUELS

First produced by the Soho Theatre Company at the Cockpit Theatre, London in 1993 and at the Vaudeville Theatre in 1996.

Between 1938 and 1939 nearly ten thousand children, mostly Jews, were sent from Germany to Britain. One of these children, Eva Schlesinger, arrives in Manchester expecting her parents to join her later. When her parents fail to escape the Holocaust she changes her name to **Evelyn** and begins the process of denying her roots. **Evelyn** is now in her fifties. Her daughter, Faith, who is about to move into a flat of her own, believes her mother to be an ordinary middle-class English woman, until searching through the attic she comes across letters and photographs belonging to 'Eva'. She questions her grandmother who finally admits that 'Eva' and **Evelyn** are one and the same person. Faith is angry and hurt and quarrels bitterly with **Evelyn**.

In this scene **Evelyn** is tearing up papers in the attic, trying to remove every trace of her past. Faith confronts her again, demanding that **Evelyn** tells her everything about her childhood in Germany and in particular, her parents.

Published by Nick Hern Books, London

Evelyn

Do you still want to know about my childhood, about my origins, about my parents? . . . Well, let me tell you. Let me tell you what little remains in my brain. And if I do, will you leave me alone afterwards. Will you please leave me alone? . . .

My father was called Werner Schlesinger. My mother was called Helga. They lived in Hamburg. They were Jews. I was an only child. I think I must have loved them a lot at one time. One forgets what these things feel like. Other feelings displace the original ones. I remember a huge cone of sweets that I had on my first day of school. There were a lot of toffees.

(She goes blank for a moment.)

I remember lots of books. Rows and rows . . . a whole house built of books and some of them were mine. A storybook filled with terrifying pictures . . . children's fingers being cut off, children whose teeth fall out and choke them while they're asleep, children being burnt in attic rooms and no one hearing them scream . . . Flames. Little flames flickering in a holder with lots of arms. Silver arms and one twisted, rocking leg holding them up. Old and faded. Rubbed away in patches. Wobbly candles which wouldn't stand straight, sticking out at strange angles. And one time . . . only once . . . being allowed to light them. Even striking the match myself. Just one, single time. And keeping watch while they melted to nothing in case they burned the house down . . . which would have been my fault because I lit them. The candles were all different colours. The little lights were the most beautiful . . . Silly lights . . . Silly, silly lights . . . . . .

The only other thing is a boy with a squint on the train I came away on. I kept trying not to look at him. Please believe me, Faith, there is nothing else in my memory from that time. It honestly is blank.

Cheryl – Irish, 22

THE KINDNESS OF STRANGERS TONY GREEN

First produced at the Everyman Theatre, Liverpool in 2004.

Set in Liverpool, each character has their own story and through-out the action these stories gradually become interlocked. Among them are Macey, a working girl trying to bring up her three children, Mohammed, a Kurdish refugee; Cliff, a waiter and a student; Jimmy, a bistro owner; and Sam, a ruthless landlord with his muscle man, Marvin. Then there is **Cheryl**, a young student and a violinist. She tells everyone she is on a gap year, but she is seriously agoraphobic and painfully thin. She is running out of money and too ill to find herself a job. Her landlord is threatening her with eviction.

In this scene, **Cheryl** and Jimmy are sitting in Cliff's kitchen waiting for him to return. They have just finished a meal and there are two empty wine bottles on the table. **Cheryl** is clutching the third botle and a glass. She is very drunk.

Published by Oberon Books, London

Cheryl

... but we're *meant* to be a talkative people, aren't we? Us Irish. We are. It's in our genes or something. We're famed for it. The world over. Yakety-yak. We love the craic. Ah, we do, we do, we do. Go on, go on, go on. Would yer just listen to us talk our lives away. Why, we live for the craic. It's better than food. Sit down love, join in the craic. Hello there, fella, join the group why don't yer? Tell us yer life story. *(Drinks.)* And where I come from, how yer talk is who yer are ... 'Ah, Brendan Flaherty, now he's a lovely fella, what a way with words he has.' And it's all bollocks, 'cause Brendan Flaherty's a lying, cheating little gobshite. He is. And would yer just listen to him playing up the lilt whenever there's an English girl nearby. Like some feckin' eejit in some stupid Hollywood film. I swear to Jesus he said 'top o' the mornin'' once. *(Drinks.)* He likes the English girls does Brendan Flaherty. And d'yer want to know why? Shall I'll tell yer why? I'll tell yer why. But keep this under yer hat. Yer might not know this, but English girls are sluts. That's right. Out and out sluts. All of them. Just mad for the sex they are. This is what Brendan thinks 'cause this is the pearl of wisdom passed down to Brendan by his great feckin' red-nosed loon of a Da. English girls are sluts and Irish girls are all ... apprentice nuns.

(She drinks, tops up her glass.)

This is exceptionally good wine ... isn't it? ... Isn't it? ... Isn't it though? Where was I? ... Oh yeah, talking. I was never one for the talking. I don't trust talky people with their gobs running away with them and their brains always struggling to catch up ... this endless torrent of meaningless words ... this ... this ... this ... this ... this relentless stream of utter *shite* ... and I come to Liverpool and I'm thinking, great, a change from Dublin ... and *it's worse!* They *never* shut up. It's like ... it's like they're so desperate to *be* Irish they're trying to outdo us or something. And everyone, I'm telling yer, *every*one in this city is a feckin' comedian. This fella, this fella down at the college, he took to calling me Marcel ... because I was so quiet. Yer know, Marcel Marceau. Oh, how he laughed at that one. *(Scouse accent)* 'All right, Marcel. How's it goin' Marcel? Been stuck in any glass boxes lately Marcel?' Prick.

(She drinks, tops up her glass.)

Mrs Mumford
NEW BOY WILLIAM SUTCLIFFE
ADAPTED FOR STAGE BY RUSSELL LABEY

First performed at the Pleasance Theatre, Edinburgh in 2000 and subsequently at the Pleasance Theatre, London in 2001.

When a new boy joins the sixth form at a North London Grammar School, seventeen year old Mark decides to take him under his wing. Barry has 'the face of an angel and the body of a Greek god' – but he is also a virgin. Mark puts the word out to the local girls' school and by the following evening Barry has slept with the best looking girl in North London. By the start of the Lent term it is evident that schoolgirls are far too easy for Barry and Mark decides he needs a more serious challenge. He compiles a list of older women working at the school, from the kitchen staff to the teachers and finally selects **Mrs Mumford**, the French teacher, as a likely target. Mark takes Barry through every step of the planned seduction and by the summer term Barry and **Mrs Mumford** have become lovers.

In this scene **Mrs Mumford** is in her classroom writing on the blackboard. She stops and stares at it for what seems like an eternity and then turns to face the class.

Published by Amber Lane Press, Charlbury, Oxfordshire

Mrs Mumford

I am aware of certain rumours circulating in the sixth form about a sexual relationship between myself and Barry. These rumours are not only potentially damaging to myself, my career and my family, they are also ... *(pause)* ... true. I am, I must admit, having an affair – an extremely passionate affair – with one of my students. I realise that this could result in my getting the sack, and I have tried to terminate our relationship, but – well – when I see him ... *(long pause)* ... and his beautiful face, I just can't turn him away.

When he touches me, I can't resist him. It feels so good – it makes me feel young. . . . Listen – listen – I deserve a bit of happiness. I am fed up with ... with all the shit. I have had enough of working twice as hard as all the other teachers in this place, who are all, of course, lazy men. . . . Yes – I'm still going to mark your essays, but I'm not going to cover them in comments you can't even be bothered to read – yes – I'm still going to look after my kids, but I'm not going to cook every fucking mouthful that ever crosses their fat, spoiled lips – and no – my husband can just go screw. So I have moved out and I am living with Barry, who I love, and who is kind to me.

I'm sorry – I didn't mean to go into all of that. I hope I haven't embarrassed you all – but I think you understand what I mean. What I wanted to say was just this – I am having an affair with Barry, and if these rumours spread to the staff, I'll get the sack, so I'm asking you a favour. I want you, my favourite class, to kill the rumours for me. Only a few people know at the moment, and I'm sure that between you, you know who they are. I want you to explain to them my situation – I want you to tell them what I have told you. This is the only time I have ever been so honest in my whole life. I would never have thought it possible that I could be so happy. Please, explain to people my situation – I need this job if I want to live without my husband. I hope you understand. I know I shouldn't trust you, but you are Barry's friends, so I'm taking a gamble. If you're anything like Barry, I know I'm safe. Thank you – thank you for helping me. I'll go now so you have some time to think about it.

Joanie – Irish, early 20s
OUR LADY OF SLIGO SEBASTIAN BARRY

Produced by the Royal National Theatre and Out of Joint and performed on the Cottesloe stage of the Royal National Theatre in 1998.

The action takes place in 1953 in a private room in Jervis Street Hospital, Dublin where Mai O'Hara lies dying, attended by a young nursing sister. 'Fuelled by alcohol, passion and despair it is the story of her flamboyant but destructive relationship with her husband Jack, the lost country of her childhood and unfulfilled expectations in the wake of Irish Independence and self rule . . . '

At the opening of the play the Nursing Sister announces that Mai has visitors – her husband, Jack and daughter, **Joanie**. Mai has recently been given a shot of morphine. Her mind is adrift with memories of the past, and as they enter she is calling out of the window for her dead father. She is persuaded to get back into bed, but the visit is a disaster, as she raves at Jack and upsets the Nursing Sister. Jack leaves. **Joanie** is about to follow him but Mai begs her to stay.

In this scene the Sister administers another injection as **Joanie** speaks.

Published by Methuen Publishing, London

Joanie

(Composed, gently) Handsomest woman in Galway in her day, Daddy says.

There she is, after embarrassing Papa and embarrassing the poor Sister and she has always been good at that. Needle, knife, and blade. And I'd be in Woolworth's with her in Sligo, getting the sheet music as may be, and she might spot a little girl, a little hungry waif of a creature like you'd see all about Sligo then, the unkillable infants of the poor, Papa called them, and I'd be there dressed to outclass Shirley Temple, a goose in a swan's coat. And she'd see the little child staring at the sweets, and she'd put thruppence into the little ruined hand, a hand like a patch of garden gone weevily, and I'd go puce with shame, puce, like one of those blood oranges Papa favoured, with shame and embarrassment, but Mammy wouldn't feel a twinge. *(To* Mai.*)* Sure you wouldn't? Impervious, imperial. The poor were there to give thruppences to. And that's why she hates Granny, Granny was a seamstress in the Sligo lunatic asylum when she was a girl in the long ago and it has never been perfectly clear and above board who her real parents were. Below buttermilk and taties. Mammy's nightmare, tea at her mother-in-law's. And one time she bought a clay pipe for an urchin, for blowing bubbles with, a clay pipe for a scrap that had never eaten meat in its life, and I died that day, yes. What did she think she was doing? And the knickers she buys for me, she has a sort of absence there on the subject of knickers, and never enough of them, so they wash, in the course of the years, into things like grey ears, big grey ears of elephants, to the point where I'm in dread of a car accident, for terror of the witnesses seeing my shameful knickers. You wouldn't show them to a nun. And when I go walking with a boy, though it's rarely, I keep a grip on my skirt like the vice of God, for fear of it lifting in the wind. Though her knickers are silk, with stuff like a pool of the cleanest water . . . A gap in her understanding. . . Mammy of the gaps. *(She goes.)*

Lady Onola – African, middle-aged
OROONOKO APHRA BEHN
A NEW ADAPTATION BY 'BIYI BANDELE

This new adaptation of Aphra Behn's novella was first performed by the Royal Shakespeare Company at The Other Place, Stratford-upon-Avon in 1999.

It tells the story of a young African Prince, Oroonoko, who is tricked into slavery, separated from his love, the Princess Imoinda and transported to the British Colony of Surinam in South America, where he is persuaded to lead a slave revolt.

In this early scene, set in the King's palace in Coramantien, Oroonoko has just arrived back from the war. He asks for an audience with the King, his Grandfather, but Oromba, the King's Chief Adviser tells him that there is nothing he can do for him as His Highness is 'attending to eminently urgent affairs of the state'. At that moment the **Lady Onola**, a middle-aged courtesan enters. She is the outspoken ex-mistress of the King and is allowed to remain at court as she is the one person who is not afraid to tell His Highness – or anyone else – the truth.

Published by Amber Line Press, Charlbury, Oxfordshire

Onola

Affairs of the state? Did you say
Affairs of the state?
(To Oroonoko.*)* What Chief Orombo means is that His
Highness our dear King is keeping
His visitors waiting while he attempts
To insert his Royal Privilege
Into the comely virtues of a young maiden.
Much ado – dare I say – over nothing.
Were the King's penis a warrior – he
Wishes it were – it would have been beheaded
Long ago for persistent dereliction of duty. . . .
It is well known in the seraglio
That though the King never can
Sleep, his penis is forever nodding off. . . .
Your wives may have slept with a snake,
Chief Orombo, but not with the one
Between the King's legs. It is a worm
Bereft of limb, flattered into thinking
Itself a reptile. . . .
I did tell your second wife, Kemi, when she said
She was marrying you that you had not
Done badly by her, for she is beautiful and
So is her smile. You bedecked her with gold and bales
Of cloth. But I could see, from looking at you,
That you could not satisfy her in bed. What
She needed in bed – I told her – was a man who once he
Mounted her would not let off until the roof fell
Through. Not a glorified pimp who farms out
His wives and children to curry royal favour.

Gabriella Pecs –30s
PENTECOST DAVID EDGAR

First performed at The Other Place, Stratford-upon-Avon in 1994 and in London at the Young Vic in 1995. Described as the first serious response in the British theatre to the tragedy of Sarajevo and a political parable, this play takes place in an unnamed South-Eastern European country.

Gabriella Pecs, art curator of the National Museum, has discovered a partly exposed painting on the wall of an abandoned church. The painting is similar to that of Giotto's *Lamentation* in the Arena Chapel, Padua and could be not only of great value, but might possibly change the history of Western art. **Gabriella** wants to remove the painting to the museum for safe-keeping and English art historian, Oliver Davenport agrees to help her. Their activities are questioned first by the Minister for Conservation of National Monuments and then by American art historian, Leo Katz who has been brought in as an expert witness. Eventually they are ordered to abandon their work, but before they can leave the church they are taken hostage by a group of refugees who demand citizenship and work permits in exchange for their release.

In this early scene **Gabriella** explains to Anna Jedlikova, the presiding Magistrate called in by Oliver, why it is imperative to remove the painting at this time. She is working from notes handed to her by Oliver; she is nervous but determined.

Note: The language of the 'country' used in the play is Bulgarian – although the country is not Bulgaria.

Published by Nick Hern Books, London

Gabriella

Um – Respected magistrate. We drag you here today for two – three reasons. First to show how this procedure to transfer painting – which you may hear accused to be a yanking off or ripping off or skinning off or flaying – is actually technique developed in middle ages and used to great effect for all time since. . . .

(She looks at Leo, *challengingly.)*

However, we also want show you *reason* for transferral. For though painting has survive so many century of candle-grease and sprinkling of holy water, shaking cause by bells – . . . What may be it cannot endure so well is to end up half way from zinc smelting works to major international autoroute. Particularly as painting faces back on autoroute and has one layer of brick remove. . . .

(Slight pause. Gabriella *is alarmed by* Leo's *silence but decides to plough gamely on.)*

So, question obviously remain as to why this painting matter. It unheard of. Anonymous. As you see from photo, not in excellent condition. But there is quite enough to tell that very similar to fresco of Italian master Giotto, painted in thirteen hundred five. With main difference that lady from behind is rock, and St John instead of throwing arm back in gesture of despair, leans one arm forward as if to comfort Virgin in her grief. And this is naturally all kind of error you must make if you are drawing from a drawing, or else out of memory.

(Leo recognises the quotation from his own remark.)

Except. Except we think that it is not this look like Giotto but that Giotto look like this. And if we are right, then it – fountainhead of next 600 years. To coin phrase, starting shot of great race to change Europe out from state of childish mediaeval superstition into modern rational universal man.

(Slight pause.)

And you know such progress can seem less big deal, if you go through your renaissance and enlightenment, if you have your Michelangelo and Mozart and Voltaire. Maybe if you reach to journey's end then it bit more easy to say, actually, this being grown up maybe not so hunky-dory after all. But, for us, it is maybe bit different. For us, being child not so far back. For those who stand on Europe's battlements since all of last 600 years.

(Pause.)

And yes it probably was painted here by foreigner. But maybe too you understand what it is meaning to us if despite all Turkish occupation, despite Mongol yoke, still this painting made, and wanted, asked for, and appreciated here. Maybe then we may feel bit more universal, bit more grown up, maybe even bit more European.

Barbs – Glaswegian, 39
PERFECT DAYS LIZ LOCHHEAD

First performed at the Traverse Theatre, Edinburgh in 1998 and revived at the Hampstead Theatre, London in 1999.

Barbs Marshall is a celebrity hairdresser working in Glasgow. She has her own show on local television and lives in a trendy apartment that she has designed herself. She is successful, but it is not enough. She is separated from her husband who has found himself a new girlfriend, and is approaching her thirty-ninth birthday.

In this opening scene she has just finishing cutting her friend Alice's hair, as she describes in detail her latest romantic disaster.

Published by Nick Hern Books, London

Barbs

So, Alice, I was telling you, we get to Glasgow airport, guy on the desk recognises me, we get an upgrade, very nice, thank you very much, First Class practically empty, great, spread out a bit, relax, the champagne cocktails, the blue blue sky, the white fluffy clouds beneath us . . . I'm feeling: OK maybe he's not got the highest IQ in the world but he does have a gorgeous profile and at least he's not wearing that fucking awful jumper that he turned up in wan night, tucked into his trousers can you believe, and gave me a red neck in front of Brendan from work.

I mean true and everlasting love it is not, but he's a nice guy and all that, own teeth, daft about me, well so far, it's only been three or four weeks, defin-ately dead keen, or so I've been led to believe by the dinners, the phonecalls, the nipping my heid about Paris – how he used to live there how there are all these sweet wee dinky little special places he knows that he'd like to take me, so there we are, we get to the hotel and here they've overbooked so this time we get an automatic upgrade to the four star no problem, it's gorgeous, the corner room, the fruitbowl, the flowers, the complimentary chocolates, the half bottle of champagne, the big kingsize bed all turned down at the corner . . . And – now, to let you know, Alice – back home in Glasgow I've been avoiding it, by the way, because truth to tell I do not really fancy him, at least I do not fancy him when I am actually *with* him, I've been, frankly, postponing the inevitable for this weekend where I have calculated, quite correctly according to my Predictor Kit, I will be *ovulating* – and he says to me he can't sleep with me because he's Met Someone and he's fallen in love! No, correction, he can *sleep* with me, but we can't have sex because that would be him being unfaithful to his new wee dolly inamorata.

I'm like: What? I'm like: What are we doing here? And Why? He's like: well, it's a fantastic city, and I'm his best friend – best friend! – and he wants to show me it and he didn't want to disappoint me!

Sarah – 30s

A PLACE AT THE TABLE SIMON BLOCK

First performed at the Bush Theatre, London in February 2000.

The action takes place in the Board/Conference Room of a small television production company, where ideals and artistic integrity are quickly elbowed for success and 'a place at the table'. **Sarah Slater** is a script editor. Her success depends on developing an idea for a new and 'very different' series to impress James, her Head of Department. She has discovered Adam, a young writer who has just had a play produced with a disabled character in the central role, but he is not prepared to sacrifice his ideals for a TV soap and has walked out on her. Five months later he returns, having completed six whole episodes, based on his play – but it is too late. A new comedy series is in the pipeline. He accuses **Sarah** of using people to further her own career.

In this scene **Sarah** explains that she can no longer support lost causes. She was even unable to help her friend, Kate, when she lost her job and was escorted out of the building.

Published by Nick Hern Books, London

Sarah

Since we last met a lot of comedy water has flowed under a lot of comedy bridges, Adam. . . . Look. When Kate was walked out of this building five months ago she was begging me to help her. I wanted to say something. Call something comforting as she was escorted to the emergency stairwell. But a voice in my head said *'enough'. 'Enough lost causes. Don't you dare move so much as a muscle'. (Beat.)* And then I returned to this room and found you'd gone too. *(Beat.)* That was more or less the final straw. . . . Having eluded it for so long I wanted to know what success at least *felt like* before I cleared my desk. If only someone else's. The crates of James' awards were over there. I remember unpacking them, and carefully lining them up on the carpet in a neat row. And as I moved along the row, reading the plaque on each – imagining my name in place of James' – I discovered . . . I discovered and *realised* at the same moment . . . . . . All the awards were for the same show. In my haste to genuflect before his prestige I had overlooked – no. I had *failed to register* the significance in the fact that he wasn't trailing a *string* of successes behind him. Only the *one*. But you land the big prize the little ones will surely follow. Topping a television festival in Germany. Winning a viewer's poll in Prague. Not a *repeated* success. Just one, and its echo. . . . The discovery made me realise James wasn't some media *sensation*. Merely flesh and blood running as far as his single stroke of luck would take him. So when I looked at James afresh, I understood it wasn't his success I coveted. But that *ease with himself* his success had engendered. And I understood that I needed to feel at ease with *my* self more than I needed to keep chasing the world with a match and gasoline. More than anything else, in fact. . . . They can call it what they like. They haven't been trying to be me for 36 years. *(Turns to the window and looks through the blind.) (Beat.)* From up here you can see half of London. Every house and flat. Every bedsit and maisonette. Every front room, lounge and kitchen. Every bedroom and study. Televisions in every one. *(Beat.)* From this window you can see half the television sets in London. *(Facing Adam.)* And if just half of those are tuned into our not especially good, but not altogether awful humourless comic on a regular basis – well – my name might finally take root somewhere. *(Beat.)* Is that such a terrible thing to want, Adam?

Lisa – London, 17

THE POWER OF THE DOG ELLEN DRYDEN

First performed at The Orange Tree Theatre, Richmond in 1996.

Vivien Chadwick, Head of the English Department in a failing school run by an incompetent Headmaster, is preparing to take up a new appointment as Head of a school in South London. At the same time she is attempting to move house as well as visit her mother who has suffered a stroke. Added to these problems is **Lisa**, a brilliant but difficult sixth-former, who she is encouraging to stay on at school and try for a place in university.

In this scene Vivien is in her study waiting for **Lisa** to arrive for an extra tutorial. **Lisa** turns up late as usual with the same old excuses – waiting thirty-five minutes for the bus and Mum being stroppy. Vivien asks if there is any chance of Mum coming to see her.

Published by First Writes Publications, London

Lisa

Nah! She doesn't like schools. Give her panic attacks. *(Pause.)* And I don't want you to come to my house. . . .

(Lisa turns her back. Then changes the subject with great energy.)
Listen. I reckon you owe me ten quid. I went to see that Midsummer Night's Dream. It was crap! Helena was about thirty-five, kept chucking herself all over the place – tossing her hair back and flinging her arms about. You know – just like young people always do when we're in love. Nearly ruptured herself. She was about six inches shorter than Hermia as well, so she'd got these gross high heels and Hermia had to bend at the knees all through the quarrel scene. And the Mechanicals wandered about in the audience and talked to us. I hate that! And Peter Quince sat in the Stalls and shouted his lines from there. And the fairies all lived in cardboard boxes and had tattoos. Puck was a drug-pusher. And it went on for nearly four hours. I reckon ours was better. And I couldn't afford it! . . . Hey and guess what! Theseus and Hypolita played Oberon and Titania! Isn't that original? Everybody liked it except me. I wanted to get up and kill them all. Bunch of tossers. . . . It was everything you say was wrong – . . . I really love that play . . . I don't think this had any . . . respect. And it wasn't – magic . . .

(She stops, lost in thought for a moment.)
I know. 'The best in this kind are but shadows and the worst no worse if imagination amend them . . . It must be your imagination then and not theirs.'

(She is very still. Her face becomes a mask.)
(Very quietly.) I like – magic. *(Briskly.)* I suppose I'm talking rubbish – everybody else says it's brilliant. And they're paid to be in the imagination business, aren't they? And I've got no right to criticize them.

Vivien – 40s
THE POWER OF THE DOG ELLEN DRYDEN

First performed at The Orange Tree Theatre, Richmond in 1996.

Vivien Chadwick, Head of the English Department in a failing school run by an incompetent Headmaster, is preparing to take up a new appointment as Head of a school in South London. At the same time she is attempting to move house as well as visit her mother who has suffered a stroke. Adding to her problems is Lisa, a difficult but brilliant student, who has been coming to her for extra tutorials. A colleague, Richard Shaw, has called **Vivien** urgently at her mother's cottage to say that her study has been broken into and the contents vandalised. Everything points to Lisa, who is resentful because **Vivien** neglected to tell her she was leaving.

In this scene Richard is helping her to clear up the study. **Vivien** is hurt and angry, but determined not to report the matter.

Published by First Writes Publications, London

Vivien

(Biting her lip.) Yes all right. I am angry. I am – hurt. Let down. I'm feeling pretty petty . . . And it's all my fault, isn't it? I picked out a little – guttersnipe – and tried to change her life. Very presumptuous. Meddling, interfering, insensitive, boneheaded *do-gooder*. Using her to make me feel good. I've got what I deserve, haven't I? I suppose I expected her to know the rules – to behave like a nice, well-mannered, *(With loathing)* grateful little middle-class miss with just a few working-class rough edges that exposure to my superior culture could smooth away! It won't do her any good to be charged with criminal damage will it? *(With a little laugh of self disgust.)* She's pretty damaged already isn't she? . . . And I – have done my best to . . . damage her even further. And I don't want the humiliation. . . . End of experiment. Once I've cleared out of here I'll stick rigidly to the rules.

  (She is rigid with tension.)

(With a sudden outburst.) I'm no sodding good at people, that's my trouble! I've got all the right ideas – wonderfully perceptive about characters in books – I don't miss a nuance! *(Brightly.)* I don't know why I'm making such a fuss. All teachers have their failures, don't they? I know why she did it but I wish she hadn't done it to me. But then that's only pride. I couldn't face Mrs Parker saying, 'I told you so!' So I'll just leave this room completely blank. Wiped clean. No trace of me – or anybody else. Let's face it, by half term everybody will have forgotten me. And if Lisa doesn't turn up everyone will breathe a collective sigh of relief. After all, it doesn't rate very high on the scale of atrocities, does it? Burning a few books. Not compared with knifings in the playground and drug-pushers at the gates. *(With a little laugh.)* I've been pushing the really dangerous drugs haven't I?

Rita – Welsh, 20s

A PRAYER FOR WINGS SEAN MATHIAS

First presented at the Edinburgh Festival at the Scottish Centre in 1985 and later transferred to the Bush Theatre, London.

The action takes place in an old church that has been poorly converted into a dwelling on the outskirts of Swansea, where **Rita** lives with her invalid mother. Every day she has to wash, dress, shop, cook for her and help her in and out of her wheelchair. Unemployment is high and she can't get a job. Her only break in the monotony is touching up the boys down at the Labour for a few shillings and sometimes bringing them back to her upstairs bedroom to earn a bit more. She prays for a 'handsome man with real manners'. If she had wings she could fly away.

In this scene it is early morning. **Rita** is sitting up in bed and her mother is calling out to her.

Published by Amber Lane Press, Charlbury, Oxfordshire

Rita

I'm having extra five minutes.
   (Pause.)
All right?
   (Pause.)
That be all right?
   (Silence.)
(Aside.) Sod her, 'cos I am anyway. . . . To tell the truth, I don't feel like getting up at all today. I could quite happily lie here in bed all day long. Under the covers. What's there to get up for? Let's be honest, now. What is there? All she thinks about is her bleeding stomach. She's not like a woman with illness. She's like a woman on bleeding holiday. Oh, I wouldn't half mind a holiday myself. Never been on holiday. I'd travel far, I can tell you. Tell you where I'd go, well, where I'd like to go. I'd like to go to America. Land of sunshine and something, isn't it? I'd go on the Q.E.2. To America. Have a big luxurious cabin. They'd be running round me. All them stewards. I'd have kippers in the morning and that fizzy wine with orange in. Champagne. That's it. I'd say, 'Bring me a magnum.' That'd keep me going. And I'd be lying there. Lying in peach satin. I'd have my hair all curly. My lifestyle would be very executive. That's the word, isn't it? Down the Job Centre you see that sometimes. Executive Posts. I bet you get a lot of trimmings in an execu-

tive post. And we'd sail into New York. And there'd be a big car to meet me. An executive car. Take me to some nice hotel. A hotel that had a door that went round and round. I've never been in one of them. I've only been up the escalators once. That was in the Co-op in Swansea. Mam says David Evans have got a lift. But we never went in there. Too dear, she says. Mind you, they got a lift down the D.H.S.S., but it stinks. Stinks of piss. I prefer the stairs myself. And a man would say, 'Let me take your luggage, madam.' I'd have twelve suitcases, 'cos I'd go to so many parties. Go out dancing. The cinema. I'd have a different frock for every film I saw. And people'd come to see me in my hotel room. A suite, isn't it? They calls it a suite. When it's in a hotel. Only suite I've seen was down the Co-op. Three piece suite, brown and beige. Mam fancied it. Contemplated H.P. I said, 'H.P.! We haven't got enough for bleeding rent.' And I'd have a big bed. Bigger than this, mind. A king size. Or maybe queen even. I'd lie on it all right. Towels by my side. Dry my locks. Oh, there's a trip I fancies, mind. There's a trip I'd go on. . . . I wonder if New York's bigger than Swansea. Big as Cardiff, maybe. Bet it is. Bet it's bigger than Sheffield, bigger than Manchester, Liverpool even. I bet it's bigger than Birmingham, Bangor, Llandudno, Aberystwyth, Brecon, Haverfordwest, Milford Haven, Builth Wells. Bigger than Neath, that's for sure. . . . Aye, waiter, we'll have two Dover sole. Send them up to my suite. With half a magnum.

Lizzie – a Western State of America, 27
THE RAINMAKER N. RICHARD NASH

Produced at the St Martin's Theatre, London in 1956 and revived again in the States in the mid 1990s, *The Rainmaker* is set in a Western State of the USA on a summer day in a time of drought.

Lizzie lives on a ranch with her father and two brothers, Jimmy and Noah. It is high time she was married, but no one has loved her or even found her beautiful. She has just returned from Sweetwater, where her father had sent her hoping she might make a match with one of her Uncle Ned's six boys. The family are anxious to know how she got on, and here she describes her disastrous visit.

Published by Samuel French, London

Lizzie

Pop, let's not beat around the bush. I know why you sent me to Sweetriver. Because Uncle Ned's got six boys. Three of them are old enough to get married – and so am I. Well, I'm sorry you went to all that expense – the railroad ticket – all those new clothes – the trip didn't work. Noah, you can write it in the books – in red ink. . . .

(Lizzie kneels by her suitcase, opens it and tidies the garments in it.)

The first three or four days I was there – I stayed in my room most of the time. . . . I knew what I was there for – and that whole family knew it, too. And I couldn't stand the way they were looking me over. So I'd go downstairs for my meals – and rush right back to my room. I packed – I unpacked – I washed my hair a dozen times – I read the Sears, Roebuck catalogue from cover to cover. And finally, I said to myself: 'Lizzie Curry, snap out of this.' Well, it was a Saturday night – and they were all going to a rodeo dance. So I got myself all decked out in my highest heels and my lowest cut dress. And I walked down to that supper table and all those boys looked at me as if I was stark naked. And then for the longest while there wasn't a sound at the table except for Uncle Ned slupping his soup. And then suddenly – like a gunshot – I heard Ned junior say: 'Lizzie, how much do you weigh?' . . . *(Lizzie rises.)* I said, 'I weigh a hundred and nineteen pounds, my teeth are all my own and I stand seventeen hands high.' . . .

(Lizzie picks up the suitcase; wryly. She moves up L and puts the suitcase on the floor in the corner.)

Then, about ten minutes later, little Pete came hurrying in to the supper table. He was carrying a geography book and he said: 'Hey, Pop – where's Madagascar?' Well, everybody ventured an opinion and they were all dead wrong. And suddenly I felt I had to make a good impression, and I said: 'It's an island in the India Ocean off the coast of Africa right opposite Mozambique.' . . . *(With a wail.)* Can I help it if I was good in geography? . . . Everything was so quiet it sounded like the end of the world. Then I heard Ned junior's voice: 'Lizzie you fixin' to be a schoolmarm?' . . .

(Lizzie moves to the hassock and sits on it.)

And suddenly I felt like I was way back at the high school dance – and nobody dancing with me. And I had a sick feeling that I was wearing glasses again the way I used to. And I knew from that minute on that it was no go. So I didn't go to the rodeo dance with them – I stayed home and made up poems about what was on sale at Sears, Roebuck's.

Nicki – Bradford, 21

SHAKERS JOHN GODBER

First presented by the Hull Truck Theatre Company at Spring Street Theatre, Hull in 1984.

'Shakers' is a trendy cocktail bar where everyone wants to be seen, from the check-out girls to the chinless wonders, the yuppies and the local lads. During the course of the action four waitresses, Carol, Mel, **Nicki** and Adele switch from role to role, playing the many characters who come into 'Shakers' – and we are given a glimpse of the reality that lies behind the plastic palms and Pina Coladas.

In this scene **Nicki** has just announced that she is going to London to audition for a place at a top drama school. The other three waitresses take on the parts of 'would be Drama Students' sitting in a line of chairs waiting to be called for the audition.

There is a spotlight on **Nicki**.

Published by Warner Chappell Plays, London

Nicki

My first audition. God I'm nervous. Do 1 look nervous? Well I am. God, I'm shakin' like a leaf. I'm ready though. Got all my stuff. The expense, shit. Twenty quid return and eighteen quid to audition. Carol thinks I've got a chance and she should know. . . .

I don't know why I want to act; well I mean I do. Everybody has a dream, I suppose. I love all the old films and that. They make me feel really good somehow. And you see I'm not from a theatrical family. My dad drives a bus. . . .

Trouble is, to be honest, nobody from our end knows how to help you. I mean, I'm twenty-one and I still want to act. It's taken me three years to get an audition together. I hope I don't blow it. I've read some books and that. I'm not thick, but I think plays are boring. . . .

I watch a lot of videos. Hey I watched that *Educating Rita*. Have you seen it? Ooh it's good, but she said that *Macbeth* was great. I got a copy from the library; I think it's boring . . . Oh well, keep your fingers crossed for me, and your legs and anything else you can cross.

I'm doing a speech, but it's not from a play. . . . It is something that I've put together myself. Er . . . I've written all the words down on a bit of paper so you can test me. Yeah. Right. It's called *The Smile*. *(Pause.)* Right I'll start shall I? *(Pause.)* I'm a bit nervous, so it might be a bit shit. She'd been in hospital for about four days. She was seventy. She went into hospital for an hysterectomy; the operation had been a great success. I went to see her and she looked great, she even showed me the stitches. She's my gran, by the way. So at work, I was having a laugh and a good time. Then they rang, the hospital, said she'd had a stroke. So I went on the bus to the hospital, I felt sick, travelling all that way on a bus. She was on the sixth floor, I remember that, in a side cubicle in a ward full of old ladies. I walked into the room. My mam and dad were looking out of the window, looking across the parkland of the hospital. And my uncle and auntie were there, looking out of the window; they were crying. My gran was laid in bed; half of her face was blue and deformed, her mouth was all twisted and taut, one eye was closed. She looked at me, and tried to smile. I remember the crying in the background. She tried to speak, but said nothing. She just laid there. 'Hello gran,' I said. 'Hello. What's all this bloody nonsense about having a stroke? Eh?' And she just smiled at me. She just smiled.

Bernadette – Liverpool, 28
STAGS AND HENS WILLY RUSSELL

First produced at the Everyman Theatre, Liverpool in 1978 and set in a Liverpool Dance Hall, where Dave and Linda have decided, unknown to each other, to hold their respective Stag and Hen parties.

In this scene the evening is in full swing. Two of the stag party, **Bernadette** and her friend Carol, come hurrying from the dance hall and into the ladies cloakroom to comb their hair and freshen up their make-up. They are laughing and joking as they make fun of the boys they'd been dancing with outside.

Published by Methuen Publishing, London

(Bernadette and Carol, *laughing enter the Ladies.)*

Bernadette

Ogh . . . God! Did y' see the state of him. An' he was serious. He tried to get off with me! He was all of four foot nothin'. . . . 'Are you stayin' up?' he says to me. All three foot six of him starin' up at me. I said 'I don't know about stayin' up, don't y' think y' better sit down before y' get trodden on. . . . He just ignored everythin'. He wouldn't take no for an answer. I said to him, 'Look son, I'll let y' into a secret, it's no use tryin' it on with me, I'm a lesbian . . . '

. . . It did no good. 'That's all right', he said, 'I like a challenge.' By this time I'm dancin' away again, hopin' no-one'd see me with him. And honest to God, he's so small he kept gettin' lost. I'm just walkin' away when he appears again. 'Goin' for a drink are we?' he says, I said to him, ''Ey you'd better run along, Snow White'll be lookin' for you.' Ey, he didn't get it though. 'Oh I'm sorry', I said, 'but I thought you were one of the Seven Dwarfs.' He started laughin' then, y' know, makin' out he's got a sense of humour. 'Oh yeh', he says, 'I'm Dozy,' I said 'You're not friggin' kiddin' . . . '

(Carol and Bernadette *laugh.)*

I'm walkin' away an' he's shoutin' after me ''Ey I'll see y' in the bar, I'll be in the bar.' I said 'Yeh, an' that's the best place for you, along with every other pint that thinks it's a quart!'

Josie – London, early 30s
STEAMING NELL DUNN

First produced at the Theatre Royal, Stratford East in 1981 it transferred later that year to the Comedy Theatre, London.

It is set in a dilapidated Turkish bath in East London, where five women, **Josie**, Jane, Nancy, Mrs Meadows and her daughter, Dawn come to relax and talk through their problems and frustrations. They are looked after by the bath attendant, Vi, who is always on hand to lend a sympathetic ear. **Josie**, is a hostess working in a Topless Club. She lives with Jerry, her German boyfriend, who pays all the bills. Jane and Nancy disapprove of **Josie**'s way of life but she points out that they know nothing of her situation. It is difficult to find a decent job when you have little or no education and she needs a man to look after her.

In this scene Vi is mending a leaking pipe as Mrs Meadows and Dawn enter and go through to the changing cubicles. **Josie** comes bursting in and goes straight over to Vi. Her lip is swollen and she has been crying.

Published by Amber Lane Press, Charlbury, Oxfordshire

Josie

He's gone. Taken everything. Only thing left is one pair of shoes under the bed. He even took his towels and the toothpaste – couldn't even clean me bleeding teeth this morning. How could he have just walked out like that after fourteen months? He found out about the job. 'I can't live with you,' he says, 'You're a slut,' and he packs his stuff, rips my clothes off my back and wallops me. *(She pulls up her skirt and shows the bruises on her thighs.)* I called him a German cunt – he went mad – called me a prostitute, ripped off my clothes and hit me in the mouth. My lip's killing me! How can I go to the club like this? I've got to have excitement or I die. I looked at him last night, he asked me to go for a walk, what do I want to walk down to the river with you for I'll end drowning myself! He hated it! . . .

   (She starts crying again.)

I know you're going to tell me I ought to get myself a job and stand on my own feet, but what can I do? I couldn't stand the sort of job I could get. I couldn't stand the boredom of it, I'd go mad. I want someone to look after me! . . . He can't have just walked out like that, can he? . . . Even rolled up the carpet in the front room and took it with him. *(Crying)* What's going to happen to me now, Violet? . . .

   (Josie drops on her knees and lays her head in Violet's lap.)

I went down on my knees to him Violet. I begged him, I even said: 'I'll try and stop swearing' – I've got a terrible feeling it's come up from deep down inside me – it's a horrible feeling . . . I'm all choked up. I was going to me new job . . . He said, 'Your place is in the home' . . . 'I haven't got any money,' I said. He slung twenty pounds at me. See, my wrists are all bruised from banging my arms against the wall. . . .

The trouble is, I know it's hopeless but I want him back more than anything, I want him back.

   (Josie and Violet look up at the skylight. It is snowing.)

I've got to find a job or I'll starve.

Stevie – young-ish

STEVIE HUGH WHITEMORE

FROM THE LIFE AND WORK OF STEVIE SMITH

First performed at the Vaudeville Theatre, London in 1977.

The action takes place in the sitting room of a small semi-detached house in North London, where the play follows the life of poetess Stevie Smith from the 1950s to the 1960s and up to the time of her death at the age of sixty-nine.

Stevie Smith's tragicomic life is portrayed by means of naturalistic dialogue scenes, by her own reminiscences or comments, sometimes with the 'Man' who plays several parts and mostly with her beloved 'Aunt Lion'.

In this scene **Stevie** is sitting on the chaise, sipping her sherry and reminiscing with her Aunt about school days and the well-meaning Miss Hogmanimy, who used to give free lectures to girls of school leaving age about how B-A-B-I-E-S are born.

Published by Samuel French, London

Stevie

How lovely. Nothing nicer. Well not much. *(She chuckles.)* There was once a woman called Miss Hogmanimy, which is certainly a name you'd want to get married out of. She had a bright smile, a highly polished face and an unprovocative blouse. She was terribly wrought up over B-A-B-I-E-S and the way they're born, and she gave up her whole life to going round giving free lectures, complete with lantern slides, to young girls of school or school-leaving age. She had a special way of talking, I remember, like losing her puff in an uphill climb, a sort of breathless whisper.

I went and sat in the school chapel with the other senior girls, eager to know exactly what happened. . . . To listen to Miss Hogmanimy you'd think that knowing how B-A-B-I-E-S are born was enough to solve all the problems of adolescence. There'd be no more coming out in spots and getting self-conscious about the senior prefect, nor getting a crush on the English mistress, nor feeling proud and miserable like you do at that time, before you get grown up. She was always going on about the beauty of the human body, but I can think of a good many things a lot more beautiful. She kept saying: Oh how beautiful it all is, and how it's the holiest thing on earth, and she'd pray a prayer first of all, and we waited and waited and hoped we'd get the facts, but no it was all this funny breathless whisper. Being all tied up with love and religious sentiments, it was just impossible for her to get the medical side of the question across; she'd draw sections on the blackboard and stand her stout body in front of it, blushing furiously. The upshot of it was she wanted us to sign a paper saying that we'd never drink anything but ginger beer and kola and allied liquids. . . .

Poor woman, she tried hard but her wits were fuddled. I came away from the lecture with a profound aversion to the subject and a vaguely sick feeling when I heard of friends and relatives about to produce offspring. I used to pray for them and wash my hands of it, though at the same time I had plenty of deep down hopes that I wouldn't end up *intacta* like one of those depressed females that never get asked, never get the chance, and go around reeking with their unholy continence. As I grew older I guessed that copulation was probably first class fun, but I'd no idea how one actually set about it, nor indeed how one ever managed to find oneself a suitable mate.

Tina – America, 45-ish
THE STRIP PHYLLIS NAGY

First performed at the Royal Court Theatre in 1995, it follows the fortunes of Ava Coo, a female impersonator, a love-struck repossession man and an obsessive lesbian journalist, as they cross America in search of fame and self gratification at the Luxor Hotel, Las Vegas. Meanwhile, in Earls Court, an astrologer, a family of white supremacists and a gay pawnbroker set off to Liverpool in search of justice. Moving amongst them all is the mysterious Otto Mink.

In this scene, set in the Ladies room of the 'Tumbleweed Junction', Las Vagas, Ava Coo's mother, **Tina** is on her hands and knees scrubbing the floor. She has a scrubbing brush in one hand and a small dictaphone, belonging to her employer, Mr Greene (alias Otto Mink) in the other. She is recording a message for Ava.

Published by Methuen Publishing, London

Tina

Dear Ava. I probably didn't get your last letter because when I married Mr. Marshall, I moved house. Not that my split level wasn't nice enough for us but . . . well now I live on a one-hundred and fifty acre ranch with Mr. Marshall. And before that, I was so busy at the casino I was hardly ever home to get my mail. But I know you wrote to me, Ava. And I know what you wrote about because let's face it honey, all our letters say the same thing. The weather is good, the weather is bad, and so on. I put pen to paper and I find myself writing the same old things, who knows why. So I am sending you a tape in the hope that it will change our routine. Mr. Marshall gave me this Dictaphone as a wedding gift and you know I've always been a freer talker than a writer. You would like Mr. Marshall. He's tall and rarely speaks. But he opens doors for me and buys me bunches of daisies from the Seven-Eleven and really, Ava, that's more than good enough. I miss your voice, honey. It's hard being a casino supervisor in Vegas, but it's rewarding. As you can imagine, I don't make many friends on the gaming floor, but I am a fair boss and last week I got Dolly Parton's autograph. Mr. Marshall breeds horses. I keep an eye out for promising colts. So far there's no hint of a Secretariat, but his horses are strong and good looking. Like him. I am babbling and so I better get to the point of this letter which is: I think I saw your daddy's picture in a newspaper last week. I say I think it was him because I haven't seen him in twenty years but it looked just like him. Except in the newspapers his name was Marquette and he looked much thinner than when I knew him. I think he killed twenty-seven people at a truck stop in Lynchburg. Well. That's all for now. I hope you are still enjoying success as a cabaret singer. I am so proud of you, Ava. With love, your mother, Mrs. Tina Coo Marshall.

(Otto *enters.*)

You're not supposed to be in here, Mr. Greene. This is the ladies room. . . . We're, uhm, running out of extra strength Lysol. . . . I had to bring some from home today. Will we be getting it on delivery any time soon? . . . I can't clean the toilets without it.

Polyxena – young
TANTALUS JOHN BARTON

First performed at the Denver Center for the Performing Arts in October 2000 and transferred to the Barbican Theatre, London in May 2001 after a short tour. *Tantalus* is the epic tale of the Trojan War, described as 'a crusade which became a catastrophe'. It is divided into three parts, *The Outbreak of War*, *The War*, and *The Homecoming*, and is made up of ten plays, one of which is *Odysseus*.

In this play Troy has been overthrown and King Priam slain. Queen Hecuba and the Trojan Women have been taken captive. At the opening scene they are all sitting or lying around the fire as Odysseus enters with his soldiers bearing food. He treats them kindly, commiserating on the death of their king and the burning and looting of Troy, which he excuses as an unavoidable 'mistake'. He explains that they have, as is the custom, been chosen, as 'war prizes'. He himself has chosen Hecuba – not for his bed – but to protect her as she once saved his life. Neoptolemus, the slayer of Priam will have two 'prizes', one for himself and one for his dead father, Achilles. This second choice has fallen on Hecuba's daughter, **Polyxena**. Hecuba protests wildly, but Odysseus replies that he has no say in the matter. **Polyxena** tells her mother to be quiet. She knows that to be the prize of a dead man means human sacrifice and explains why she is prepared to die.

Published by Oberon Books, London

Polyxena

You must stop this, mother;
Be quiet and listen to me.
After Achilles died
Cassandra told me what would happen
But I shut it out of my mind
As you are trying to do now.
Quiet, Mother. You have spoken
Fine words about the future
Because it's against the rules
For those who govern kingdoms
To dare to speak the truth.
You left out the one word that matters:
We are slaves. Each one of you

Will scrub floors and be whipped
If you do not please your masters;
You will sweat all day in the fields
And at night share some brute's bed
And his snores will mock your memories.
I would rather die than be chosen
For the bed of the butcher-boy
Who killed my dear father.

Take me to my husband
And let Calchas cut my throat;
I want that, yes, I want it:
It is said that all dead men
Love to drink the blood of the living
Because it gives them the sense
Of being alive again.
Achilles does not call for me
Because he wants revenge
But because he loves his wife.
If there had been time
For us to be together
As a man and wife should be
We would have made peace
Between Troy and the West
And I would have learned to love him.
If my blood now can give him
A little sense of life
I shall be a true wife to him. . . .
I shall see my father
Underneath the earth
And meet all my brothers
And Hector will hug me
As he did when I was little.
Why should I fear Asphodel
When at last I will be able
To tell Paris what I think of him?

Ella – 40s
THREE WOMEN AND A PIANO TUNER
HELEN COOPER

First performed at the Chichester Festival Theatre in June 2004.

Three sisters, **Ella**, Beth and Liz are bound together by a father's love for his daughter and a mother's love for her son – and the choices they made or didn't make.

After ten years **Ella** has at last completed her piano concerto and now she needs the help of Beth, married to a millionaire and Liz, a famous concert pianist to get it performed. But first they must delve back into a painful childhood. Could their mother somehow have prevented their sister Jane's death? And who is the young piano tuner working in the next room?

In this early scene **Ella** and Beth have just returned from eating out in a local restaurant. **Ella** fetches some wine. She pours two glasses and joins Beth at the kitchen table, choosing a chair that is furthest away from her. There is tension between them, as they wait for the arrival of Liz. **Ella** recalls their childhood and the oblong table which they sat around for every evening meal at six o' clock exactly. In the background they can hear the piano tuner indulging in a little prelude.

Published by Nick Hern Books, London

Ella

Oh, yes, of course, the oblong table. Every evening meal at six o'clock exactly. Every evening. And I was always worrying whether Mother would be in a good mood or not. She always was when there were guests, but when there weren't, it was grim for her to face the cruel facts: a man without ambition, four mediocre daughters, her own wild talent shrivelled up, no money, a damp, small, rented house. Even after she had covered all the cushions in desperate florals and painted the room, we ate in a deep blue, it never could pretend to be what it was not.

[Beth *looks at her diamond ring.*]

But when a guest did eat with us, then Mother's hair had curls, her lips were red, her eyes had pale blue eye-shadow. There would be alcohol and so the atmosphere would be completely different.

Then Mother would forget that her eldest daughter was considered thick, no school could teach her, that number two had a nasty temper and tendencies to mingle with a dodgy crowd, that the youngest, the mute one, slouching in a corner, simply would not eat or drink or speak and that Jane, number three, had given up playing the piano, because she felt she was grotesque, too ugly to perform in public, too off-putting to be looked at, to be seen. Jane kept begging Mother for all mirrors in the house to be removed, and finally, one day, Mother shrugged her aching shoulders in despair and stored all mirrors in the coalhole.

(Beth *lights another cigarette.)*
Couldn't Mother have prevented it? Jane's death? Couldn't she have prevented it? And what about Father?
(Ella waits for a reaction from Beth. *But there is none.)*
We all knew that Father's life was not around that oblong table. It was elsewhere but only I knew where. That was the secret and I guarded it. I knew that Mother didn't know I knew, but I knew that she suspected that I knew and I knew that that was bad enough. So I kept my mouth firmly shut and hardly ever ate or drank or spoke in the presence of my mother.
(Ella looks at Beth *smoking.)*
Mother always was embarrassed when she was asked what Father's profession was. 'He plays . . . eh . . . the viola *(embarrassed laugh)* in a small orchestra.'
(Beth does not react.)
Couldn't Mother have prevented it?
(Beth does not react.)
And yet how could it have been her fault? She tried. She always tried. She cooked and cleaned and washed and sewed. She made us practise the piano, practice, practice . . . Four daughters to bring up on the income from just one small viola in a feeble orchestra.

But of course after Jane's death, after we had all been kicked out of our oblivion and been woken up to the terror of reality, our previous poverty seemed rich.

Especially for Mother, 'Before the Fall' became a beautiful glowing island of our intimate togetherness, a kind of haven before we were all forced to sail the unknown seas.

Right up until her death, old and decrepit as she was, Mother still hankered back to that blissful paradise. But I was there, don't forget, the mute one, slouching in the corner, and I can tell you, blissful it was not.
(Beth waits for more.)
You see, that is the recurring theme. Around that oblong table every night at six o'clock.

Katherine Woodstock – 27
THROUGH A CLOUD JACK SHEPHERD

First performed in October 2004 at the Drum Theatre, Plymouth and shortly after at the Birmingham Repertory Theatre.

It is June 1656 during the last years of the Commonwealth, and certain influential men are pressuring Oliver Cromwell to become king, reigning over the country with absolute authority.

The action takes place in the woods surrounding Hampton Court Palace, where the blind poet, John Milton and his wife to be, **Katherine Woodstock** have come to meet Cromwell to discuss this situation over a picnic lunch. An unwelcome interruption by a wild man, appearing suddenly from the bushes, leads to a heated debate that 'calls into question the jaded aspirations of those in power and the utopian ideologies of those who sit on the sidelines.' Cromwell is exhausted by this encounter and we see that he is not only a very sick man but also a sad and disillusioned one.

There is an awkward pause and **Katherine** suggests she puts out their lunch. As she unpacks the picnic hamper, she talks of happiness and misery and animals feeling the same as we do. They are all God's creatures and have souls. Cromwell comments that many people would consider this an admission of heresy and not so long ago would have brought her to the stake.

Published by Nick Hern Books, London

Katherine

Shall I lay out the food? . . .

Happiness is so short-lived, isn't it? And so is misery, thank goodness. If you're sad one day, it doesn't mean to say you won't be happy the next. Yesterday, down by the river, I saw a kingfisher perched on a pole. Its feathers were still wet from skimming over the water and diving down for fish. Such a beautiful bird. I wanted to hold it. Feel its beating heart. But when I got too close, it flew away in a dazzle of blue.

(She lays three places on the grass. Each one with plate, knife, beaker and napkin.)

What makes us so special, Mr Cromwell? Who's to say the birds and the animals don't feel just like we do. And the insects too . . . Joy. Hunger. Hope and despair. Who's to say?

(Silence.)

When I was a little girl, I was told by our minister that animals didn't have souls. That only *we* have souls, we humans. And it upset me terribly. Aren't they mortal, too, I thought, just like we are? What makes us so special that God should single us out for immortality and not the rest of his creation? And for a while, I'm afraid to say, I lost my faith. It was not until I started to believe . . . Secretly believe . . . that the rest of God's creatures must have souls as well . . . that my faith began to return. And everything started to feel whole again. . . .

It's what I believed then. When I was young and innocent. But I'm a grown woman now. And I know how things go in the world.

Shona – 21
TOP GIRLS CARYL CHURCHILL

First performed at the Royal Court Theatre, London in August 1982 and transferring to Joe Papp's Public Theatre, New York later in the same year. It returned to the Royal Court in 1983.

The play has been described as a powerful exposition of the way in which top girls, like top men, often achieve success at the expense of their less able sisters.

The second act is set in the office of the 'Top Girls' Employment Agency. The interviewers, Win and Nell cherish those who might be 'tough birds' like themselves, but otherwise their tone is harsh and unfeeling.

In this scene Nell is interviewing twenty-one year old **Shona**, who appears confident and successful. She is interested in selling computers ('a top field') or video systems ('a high flying situation') and to the suggested large salary she replies blandly, 'sounds ok'. This brash confidence impresses Nell who then asks her to describe her present job.

Published by Methuen Publishing, London

Shona

What I've been doing. It's all down there. . . . I'm twenty-nine years old.
. . . We look young. Youngness runs in the family in our family. . . .

My present job at present. I have a car. I have a Porsche. I go up the M1
a lot. Burn up the M1 a lot. Straight up the M1 in the fast lane to where
the clients are, Staffordshire, Yorkshire, I do a lot in Yorkshire. I'm
selling electric things. Like dishwashers, washing machines, stainless
steel tubs are a feature and the reliability of the programme. After sales
service, we offer a very good after sales service, spare parts, plenty of
spare parts. And fridges, I sell a lot of fridges specially in the summer.
People want to buy fridges in the summer because of the heat melting
the butter and you get fed up standing the milk in a basin of cold water
with a cloth over, stands to reason people don't want to do that in this
day and age. So I sell a lot of them. Big ones with big freezers. Big
freezers. And I stay in hotels at night when I'm away from home. On
my expense account. I stay in various hotels. They know me, the ones I
go to. I check in, have a bath, have a shower. Then I go down to the bar,
have a gin and tonic, have a chat. Then I go into the dining room and
have dinner. I usually have fillet steak and mushrooms, I like
mushrooms. I like smoked salmon very much. I like having a salad on
the side. Green salad. I don't like tomatoes.

Sandie – mid 30s
TOPLESS MILES TREDINNICK

This one-woman play was first presented in London by Open Top Productions in association with the Big Bus Company in 1999 and is set on the open top of a London sightseeing bus on a summer's day.

Sandie is a tour guide on a 'fabulous' tour of London on an open top sightseeing bus. She can't wait to point out all the sights from Big Ben to the Tower of London and explain their history. Unfortunately that's not all she wants to talk about. Domestic problems and sightseeing become intertwined as she reveals how she deals with her straying husband.

In this opening scene she is reading from a clip-board in dreadful French. Nobody is listening to her and she realises something is wrong. The group she is talking to are not from Calais after all.

Published by Comedy Hall Books, London

Sandie

Bienvenue a Londres et Bienvenue chez 'London Topless Buses'. Le 'Topless' est le moyen idéal de visiter sans effort les sites touristiques de Londres. Je m'appelle Sandie et notre chauffeur est Sid .... *(She realises something is wrong and shouts down the stairwell.)* Sid? Are you sure this is the group from Calais? Because they don't seem particularly French to me. They've what? Cancelled? Oh. Well thanks for telling me. *(Facing audience.)* So you all speak English do you? Well I won't be needing that. *(She puts the clip-board down on one of the front seats.)* Hi everyone and welcome to London.

My name's Sandie and I'm your tour guide. How are you all? Everyone OK? I'm feeling absolutely brilliant today. I am. Honestly. Now I know what you're thinking. The wheel's turning but the hamster's dead. But don't worry, I haven't got going yet. I'm building up to my tour de force and believe me it'll be worth waiting for. We're going to have a fabulous tour. Now 'cos I thought you were all going to be foreign I've brought along a few *visual aids* to jazz things up a bit. *(She opens her bag and hands out various London souvenirs starting with a miniature Big Ben.)* This is Big Ben which we'll be seeing later. Who wants Big Ben? *(She then takes out a little Beefeater doll.)* And here's one of the Yeoman Warders you'll see down the Tower. *(Next she produces a policeman's helmet and puts it on a man's head.)* Evening all!

(She salutes him.) Love your helmet sir. Smashing. *(She holds up a large plastic cigar.)* And what's this one? It's Winston Churchill, ain't it. *(She hands it to someone.)* You hold that and wave it when I get to me Churchill bit. *(She then holds up something wrapped in silver foil.)* And what have we got 'ere? Oh me sandwiches. Only cheese and tomato I'm afraid. If anyone wants to do a swop later I'm game. Provided it's not meat. I'm a veggie. Right, that's the basics dealt with so off we go. *(She presses the bus bell button twice.)* Now our driver is called Sid, he's the best driver in the country. Hopeless in town but in the country he's brilliant!

(The bus starts up. It jerks off. Sandie grabs a safety rail to steady herself.)

See what I mean!! Hold on tight! Right, now I'm going to take you on a fabulous trip around London. I'm going to show you all the big sights. Trafalgar Square, Big Ben, Westminster Abbey, St Paul's Cathedral, all the way down to the Tower of London. So sit back and enjoy yourselves. If you've got any questions keep them to yourselves! I haven't got time for questions, I'll be too busy talking! I'm the original motormouth, me.

(She turns to take in the first sight.)

Right, now we're kicking off in Piccadilly.

Governess – 20s

THE TURN OF THE SCREW HENRY JAMES
ADAPTED FOR STAGE BY JEFFREY HATCHER

First performed by The Portland Stage Company in Portland, Maine (USA) in 1996 and revived at The New End Theatre, London by Modern Eyes Theatre Company in 2004. It was later performed at the Oldham Colliseum in Spring 2005.

It is set in an English country house in 1880, where a young inexperienced governess is hired to tutor two young orphans, Miles and Flora. Miles has been expelled from his boarding school as being unsuitable to mix with other boys. No further explanation has been given. Mrs Grose, the housekeeper tells the **Governess** that both children have been subjected to the influence of the previous governess, Miss Jessel and her lover, the evil Peter Quint. Both are now dead, but have reappeared as ghosts and are still exerting their influence over the children. The **Governess** discovers a bible that belonged to Miss Jessel with a riddle written in her hand on a page of Genesis, 'What comes between a man and a woman, but allows everything?'

In this scene she asks Miles what this means. He seems surprised. 'Why, miss, that's easy. A touch.' He kisses her on the lips. Their kiss holds for a long moment. Miles pulls away, smiles and goes off into the darkness. Silence. Then the **Governess**'s hand flies to her lips. She speaks out front.

Published by Dramatists Play Service Inc, New York

Governess

I open my bedroom door! In the fading light I see her. Jessel, my weeping predecessor, standing befoe me in the gloom. Dishonoured and tragic, her haggard beauty and her unutterable woe. Why do *you* weep, you terrible, miserable woman? You have defeated me! I am no heroine! I am alone and unable and *untouched! I cannot save the children, they belong to you and that devil, Peter Quint, Peter Quint!* (The Governess shuts her eyes. Then she opens them. An idea has dawned. She looks to the side.) Peter Quint. Peter Quint . . . Peter Qu . . . His Name. *Say His Name.* (The Governess looks back out front looking for Miss Jessel.) Jessel! *Jessel!* (Beat.) I must not flee. My governess has given me the clue. I know now how to save the children. . . .

I know why the spectres have come to Bly, and I know why the children have been trying to *bring them back!* . . .

Miles answered the riddle for me in the graveyard: *What comes between a man and a woman . . . but allows everything?* A *touch.* The ghosts want the children, so they can once again touch each other, enter each other, *possess* each other. But they can only possess each other by entering the children and possessing them. The children will lose their souls and become instruments of their vile physic! Miles and Flora can perform their foul deeds *for* them. In the nursery, in the garden, in – . . .

Hush, Mrs Grose. SHHHH! I must start from the outer edges of the conspiracy. . . . With Miles' school, with the crimes his headmaster dared not speak. Why was Miles expelled? Is he stupid? Is he untidy? Is he ill-natured? No. Miles is *exquisite* – so the reason can be only *evil.* And whatever evil he did there, someone taught it him. When I have discovered what crimes Miles committed at that school, I'll have Quint within my grasp.

Valerie – Irish/Dublin, 30s
THE WEIR CONOR McPHERSON

First performed at the Royal Court Theatre Upstairs in 1997 and then at the Duke of York's Theatre, London in 1998. The action takes place in present time in a bar in a rural part of Ireland – Northwest Leitrim or Sligo. Barman, Brendan, and locals Finbar, Jack and Jim, are swapping ghost stories to impress **Valerie**, a young woman from Dublin newly moved into the area. One of these stories concerning a child obviously disturbs her and she asks the way to the Ladies' cloakroom. When she returns Finbar announces that they've had enough of the stories. There must be no more of them. **Valerie** insists that she'd like to tell them something that happened to her personally, concerning her five-year old daughter who had died the previous year in an accident in the swimming pool at the Central Remedial Clinic.

Published by Nick Hern Books, London

Valerie

But, and then one morning. I was in bed, Daniel had gone to work. I usually lay there for a few hours, trying to stay asleep, really. I suppose. And the phone rang. And I just left it. I wasn't going to get it. And it rang for a long time. Em, eventually it stopped and I was dropping off again. But then it started ringing again, for a long time. So I thought it must have been Daniel trying to get me. Someone who knew I was there.

So I went down and answered it. And. The line was very faint. It was like a crossed line. There were voices, but I couldn't hear what they were saying. And then I heard Niamh. She said, 'Mammy?' And I . . . just said, you know, 'Yes.'

(Short pause.)

And she said . . . She wanted me to come and collect her. I mean, I wasn't sure whether this was a dream or her leaving us had been a dream. I just said, 'Where are you?'

And she said she thought she was at Nana's. In the bedroom. But Nana wasn't there. And she was scared. There were children knocking in the walls and the man was standing across the road, and he was looking up and he was going to cross the road. And would I come and get her?

And I said I would, of course I would. And I dropped the phone and I ran out to the car in just a teeshirt I slept in. And I drove to Daniel's mother's house. And I could hardly see. I was crying so much. I mean. I knew she wasn't going to be there. I knew she was gone. But to think wherever she was . . . that . . . . And there was nothing I could do about it.

Daniel's mother got a doctor and I . . . slept for a day or two. But it was . . . Daniel felt that I . . . needed to face up to Niamh being gone. But I just thought that he should face up to what happened to me. He was insisting I get some treatment, and then . . . everything would be okay. But you know, what can help that, if she's out there? She still . . . she still needs me.

(Pause.)

Woman – late 20s–30s
A WOMAN ALONE FRANCA RAME & DARIO FO

A Woman Alone is one of a group of monologues first performed in Milan in 1977. They were later performed at the Half Moon Theatre, London in 1989.

Although this is a consistently funny piece, it shows a housewife who has everything in the bosom of her family except the most important thing: the right to be treated by the men of the house as an individual, and respected as such, not used only as a sexual object and an unsalaried servant.

In this opening scene the **Woman** enters holding a basket over-flowing with garments to be ironed. The radio is blaring rock music. The **Woman** dancing frenetically, puts the basket on the table. She grabs a man's jacket out of the basket, and still dancing, goes towards an imaginary window at the front of the stage. She shakes the jacket as if she is trying to get dust out of it. She stops, pleasantly surprised to find someone in the flat opposite.

Published by Methuen Publishing, London

Woman

(At the top of her voice, to get attention) Hey! Hello there! Morning! How long have you been living over there? I didn't even notice you moving in . . . I thought it was empty . . . I'm thrilled to bits *(Almost shouting.)* I was saying I'm thrilled to . . . Can't hear me? Oh yeah, of course . . . the radio . . . I'll turn it off. I always have to have the radio going full blast when I'm at home on my own . . . otherwise I feel like sticking my head in the oven . . . I've always got the stereo going in this room . . . *(She opens the door. We hear music.)* Can you hear? *(Closes the door.)* And I've got the cassette machine in the kitchen . . . *(Same business at the kitchen door.)* Can you hear? *(She closes the door.)* So whatever room I'm in, I've always got company. *(She goes over to the table and begins to work: she brushes the man's jacket, sews on buttons etc.)* No . . . not in the bedroom, that'd be a bit over the top! No I've got the telly on in there . . . it's always on – I keep it turned right up! There's a church service on right now . . . they're singing . . . in Greek, I think . . . that's what Prince Philip talks, isn't it? What a weird language . . . it's all double dutch to me . . . Yeah, I like music you can't dance to as well . . . anything as long as it's music . . . the sound keeps me company. What do you do for company? Oh you've got a son! Aren't you the lucky one!

Come to think of it, I've got a son too! Actually, I've got two kids . . . Sorry, I got so excited about talking to you, I forgot about the other one . . . No they don't keep me company. The big girl's grown up. You know how it is, she's got 'friends her own age' . . . the little boy's still with me, but he's no company . . . well, he's asleep all the time! He does nothing but sleep! He poos, he sleeps and he snores! Oh I'm not moaning, I'm really well-off here in my flat . . . I've got everything I could ever want . . . My husband treats me like porcelain! I've got everything! I've got . . . O God, I've got so much . . . I've got a fridge! Yes I know everyone's got a fridge, but *(emphasising this)* mine makes round ice cubes!! I've got a washing machine . . . twenty-four programmes! It washes *and* dries . . . ooh, you should see the way it dries! Sometimes I have to wet everything again so I can iron it . . . it comes out bone dry! I've got a non-stick slow cooker . . . a Magimix with all the attachments . . . music in every room . . . what more could I ask of life? I'm only a woman after all! Yes, I used to have a cleaning lady but she ran away; then I got another one and she ran away too . . . those women all run away from my house . . . What? Oh no, not because of me . . . *(embarrassed)* It's my brother-in-law . . . Well he gropes them! He feels them up! All women! He's a groper! . . . He's sick . . . off his head? Well, I don't know if he's off his head . . . all I know is he wanted to do these things to those girls . . . and they weren't too keen – quite right too. You should see it, love. There you are, minding your own business, getting on with the housework, and suddenly oops! there's this hand right up your . . . gives you the creeps! And you should see my brother-in-law's hand! Thank God he's only got the one!

. . . becomes a mask.
(Very quietly) I like – magic. *(Briskly)* I suppose I'm talking rubbish – everybody else says it's brilliant. And they're paid to be in the imagination business, aren't they? And I've got no right to criticize them.

more ideas *for*
speeches

Sheila – early 20s

AN INSPECTOR CALLS J. B. PRIESTLEY

First performed at the Opera House, Manchester in 1946 it transferred to the New Theatre, London later that year. One of the most recent revivals was at the Royal National Theatre in 1995 and it has been touring the UK during 2005.

Set in 1912 in the dining room of a large suburban house in the North Midlands where Arthur Birling is holding a dinner party to celebrate the engagement of his daughter, **Sheila** to the son of a wealthy industrialist. They are interrupted by the arrival of Inspector Ghoul who informs them that a young girl has committed suicide and they are all in some way involved. At first the family deny all knowledge of the girl, but gradually one by one they are forced to admit their common responsibility.

In this scene **Sheila** confesses that she did know her.

Published by Samuel French, London

Act I

START: 'You knew it was me all the time, didn't you? . . .

(Omitting the Inspector's line and carrying on to:)

. . . now I feel a lot worse.'

CUT TO: 'I'd gone in to try something on . . .

TO: . . . I couldn't be sorry for her.'

CUT TO: 'I know, I know . . .

FINISH: . . . why had this to happen?'

Catwoman – Irish, 50
BY THE BOG OF CATS MARINA CARR

First performed at the Abbey Theatre, Dublin in 1998 and later at Wyndham's Theatre, London in November 2004.

It is loosely based on the Greek tragedy of *Medea*, who killed her own children to revenge herself on her husband. This early scene opens beside a caravan on the Bog of Cats in rural Ireland, where Hester Swane is digging a grave for the friend of her childhood – the black swan.

The blind prophetess, **Catwoman**, enters dressed in a long coat of cat furs. She takes the swan, kisses it and gives it back to Hester to lay it in the grave. Hester begs her to tell her about her mother – Big Josie Swane.

Published by Faber & Faber, London

Act I scene 3

START: Ya'd often hear her voice comin' over the bog at night . . .

[Omitting Hester's *next line and carrying on to:]*

. . . I started to turn again' her.'

CUT TO: 'Ya were lucky she left ya. Just forget about her and lave this place now or ya never will.'

Carla – age unknown – possibly 30s/40s
COMIC POTENTIAL ALAN AYCKBOURN

First produced at the Stephen Joseph Theatre, Scarborough in 1998 and subsequently at the Lyric Theatre, London in 1999. It is set in the near future.

Carla Pepperbloom is the Director of a commercial television company producing TV soaps using android actors. A woman of uncertain age, she is used to having her own way and has a reputation for taking up with young men, known in the company as the 'Pepperbloom Babes'. She arrives at the studio with Adam Trainsmith a young writer and nephew of the chairman, who is anxious to study television technique with Chance Chandler, a director he has long admired. Adam is fascinated by the 'actoids' and persuades Chance to let him try out an idea of his own.

Carla proceeds to teach Adam about life in television.

Published by Faber & Faber, London

Act I scene 2

START: 'Adam, dear, you badly need to learn the facts of television life . . .

(Omitting Adam's two lines and finishing:)

. . . toe the line like everybody else.'

Serafina Pekkala – Queen of the Lapland Witches
HIS DARK MATERIALS PHILIP PULLMAN
ADAPTED FOR STAGE BY NICHOLAS WRIGHT

Adapted from Philip Pullman's novels into two full length plays *His Dark Materials* was first produced at the Royal National Theatre, London in December 2003.

This is the second part of an epic tale that spreads itself across time and into strange worlds, old and new. At the centre is Lyra, described as a child of destiny, who unknown to herself has it in her power to bring about the annihilation of death and the triumph of the mysterious 'dust'. Accompanied by her friend, Will, she sets out to rescue her father, Lord Asriel from the clutches of 'The Authority'.

The Lapland Witches have sworn to protect Lyra until her destiny can be fulfilled. They have been searching for her throughout the worlds and eventually **Serafina** finds her in 'Cittagazze' – with Will, lying sick on the ground beside her.

Published by Nick Hern Books, London

Part Two Act I
START: 'It's hard for a witch to know . . .
(Omitting Lyra's *lines and* Serafina's: *'He was. And I loved him' and 'I know that' – before her final two lines.)*

FINISH: . . . like yours and this boy's may be.'

Pearl - rural, 20s

HOUSE AND GARDEN ALAN AYCKBOURN

First produced at the Stephen Joseph Theatre, Scarborough in 1999 and subsequently at the Royal National Theatre on the Lyttleton and Olivier stages in August 2000. *House and Garden* consists of two plays that can be performed at the same time on two separate stages – although each play is complete in itself. This scene is from *Garden*.

Pearl is a member of the domestic staff and could be described as a casual cleaner. She is the daughter of the housekeeper, Izzy. Both mother and daughter live with Warn, the gardener and **Pearl** spends most of her working hours bringing him his lunchbox, or fighting with her mother over him. Warn takes all this for granted.

In this scene she has just brought Warn his 'levenses.

Published by Faber & Faber, London

Garden – Act I scene 1

START: 'Here. Brought you your 'levenses . . .

TO: . . . You want to get a stick and clean it out.

(Note: This is an excellent comedy scene and runs approximately four minutes. If you need a shorter speech it can be cut quite easily, as follows:)

AT: . . . That's all I'm saying. Know what I mean?'

Or

AT: . . . I'm easy. I don't care.'

Nazreen – South Asian, 17

IN THE SWEAT NAOMI WALLACE AND BRUCE MCLEOD

This is one of the plays for young people performed at the Royal National Theatre in 1997. The action takes place in a derelict synagogue in Spitalfields, London where four young people, Fitch, Scudder, Duncan and Nazreen meet and talk. Towards the end of the play Nazreen relives the scene where her elder sister was trapped in a burning phone booth.

From New Connections – *New Plays for Young People*
Published by Faber & Faber, London

Page 367
START: 'Seven years ago. Yes. Like. Seven hundred. My sister, Mahfuza, and I, we went out to use the phone. To call for flowers . . .
TO: . . . This is it. Here. Right here, isn't it? Under our feet?'

Wanda – New York, 20
KENNEDY'S CHILDREN ROBERT PATRICK

First performed in New York City it premiered in London at the Kings Head Theatre, Islington in 1974, later transferring to the Arts Theatre in 1975.

It is set in a bar on the Lower East Side in New York City. Throughout the action the characters are thinking their own thoughts, reliving happy times and moments of despair. They never acknowledge each other or speak directly out to the audience. Drinks are bought as needed, paid for, drunk and cleared away again.

Wanda works for a fashion magazine, pasting captions onto photos. At the opening of the play she sits alone sorting through papers.

Published by Samuel French, London

Act I
START: 'For me, it was the most important day of my life . . .
TO: . . . The President's been shot in Dallas!'

Note: Wanda has other speeches that can be added to this one if needed. It is also worth looking at the characters Rona and Carla.

Allie – young
MULES WINSOME PINNOCK

First produced at the Royal Court Theatre Upstairs in 1996. Girls are needed for the drugs trade. Preferably young girls who need money, enjoy air travel and taking risks. Bridie works in the London office. Her job is to recruit the girls. Lou and Lyla were picked up in a bar in Jamaica, **Allie** in a London street. In this scene **Allie** is with Bridie in a London hotel. She has just completed her first assignment.

Published by Faber & Faber, London

Act II scene 10
START: 'All through the flight I wanted to scratch my head . . .
TO: . . . and I don't want to wake him up.'
CUT TO: 'Going through customs . . .
  (Omitting Bridie's one line and finishing:)

. . . And I was.'

Note: Bridie also has an excellent speech in scene 9 when she pretends to 'die' on stage and then goes on to describe the various forms of death she has seen in the drugs trade.